D0662096

THE JOY AND CHALLENGE OF RAISING AFRICAN AMERICAN CHILDREN

By Emma McElvaney Talbott

Black Belt Press
Montgomery

Black Belt Press
P.O. Box 551
Montgomery, AL 36101

Library of Congress Cataloging-in-Publication Data

Talbott, Emma M., 1943-
    The joy and challenge of raising African American children / by
Emma M. Talbott.
        p. cm.
    Includes bibliographical references.
    ISBN 1-881320-79-0 (softcover)
    ISBN 1-881320-90-1 (hardcover)
    1.Child rearing—United States. 2. Afro-American children.
3. Parenting—United States. I. Title.
HQ769.T267 1996
649'.1'08996073—dc2O   96-41344
                                                        CIP

DESIGN BY RANDALL WILLIAMS
Printed in the United States of America
96 97 98   5 4 3 2 1

Our appreciation is expressed to the models appearing in the photo-
graph on the front cover of this book: James Franklin, Shirley
Franklin, Ashley Franklin, and Jamaal Franklin, of Montgomery,
Alabama. Photo by Penny Weaver.

*The Black Belt, defined by its dark, rich soil, stretches across
central Alabama. It was the heart of the cotton belt. It was and
is a place of great beauty, of extreme wealth and grinding
poverty, of pain and joy. Here we take our stand, listening to
the past, looking to the future.*

To the Memory and Unconquerable Spirit of
My Parents,
David C. and Emma W. Miles McElvaney

Contents

Acknowledgments

The author acknowledges her indebtedness to her husband, Cecil, for his love, patience, and encouragement when this book was only an idea.

I would also like to acknowledge my sons, Chip (Cecil Jr.) and Chad, who "allowed" me to be their mother. They have added immeasurable joy, as well as challenges, to my life.

The support of family and friends who affirmed this project with words of support and many prayers meant a great deal.

I am grateful to Randall Williams, publisher, and the staff of Black Belt Press, for believing in this book and recognizing the need for yet another book on parenting.

Deborah Day, my editor, has been a jewel in gently guiding me through the process of turning my initial manuscript into a more polished and orderly work. Her wise suggestions served as a positive catalyst as I labored to present my most basic beliefs on raising African-American children.

My gratitude goes to the Louisville Western Branch Library staff that stood ready to assist me on numerous occasions.

And, most of all, I acknowledge the guiding force of The Absolute who is the author and finisher of my faith.

Preface:

To Black Parents

This book contains the words of one who has been a trial-and-error practitioner for three decades in "the village" efforts to successfully raise African American children. This childrearing philosophy is the product of my efforts to raise my own children and to impart knowledge and to impact the lives of thousands of children entrusted to my care by the state. It is the result of my successes and failures and my casual observation of parenting practices of friends, students' parents, parents with whom I have come in contact in various settings, and reflections of my own parents' efforts to raise six children.

Teaching children and thus standing in loco parentis for them proved to be a major and ongoing challenge. In many ways my students may have impacted my life more than I theirs. I have studied my students. I have observed their likes and dislikes. I have observed the budding genius and also the child who had to struggle for every bit of knowledge that he could acquire.

Their life stories came to school with them. Stories of drug-addicted mothers and fathers; and of fathers or sometimes mothers who were incarcerated. Young bodies and minds broken by mental, physical and sexual abuse have become all too common. Other young minds are broken and ambitions thwarted by feelings of hopelessness due to lack of concern, encouragement and belief in their abilities by those entrusted to care for and guide them.

On the other hand, I have seen the happy and contented child come to school everyday, inquisitive and ready to learn. I have seen the child come in who feels secure and loved and expects a continuation of his stable and happy home life when he enters my classroom. Too many times, these have not been the faces of African American children. We must find ways to build and secure our children's feelings of self-worth in the family and community and make certain that there is a continuation of positive reinforcement when they come to school.

It has been my good fortune to follow several of my students through high school and beyond. Many have gone on to fulfill their youthful dreams, while others have seen those dreams dashed by life circumstances or by their own poor life choices.

Parents must remember that though they may view their children as extensions of themselves, in truth, our children are separate entities. They have minds of their own and may not follow our dictates and wishes. Thus, we must guide them toward self-fulfillment on their own terms.

Children will, and often do, make mistakes. As parents, we always hope that they do not make the same mistakes that we made. Our desire is to help them avoid as many pitfalls as possible. We cannot help our children avoid all mistakes, but we may reduce the number of major mistakes by guiding and molding them at a young and impressionable age.

The contents of this book are offered as a first line of action in a crime-filled and mean society that can bring even the strong to their knees.

Some of the suggestions, practices and information offered herein will affirm and reinforce many of the positive things parents and caregivers are already doing, while other ideas may stimulate action in areas where little thought has been given.

The resource section may prove beneficial in expanding your family's knowledge of your own African American world.

The historical theme that runs throughout is based on a strong belief that if children know their history and the sacrifices, the achievements, and the joy and pain that is included, they will be less inclined to treat their lives frivolously. Instead, they will build on a foundation that has been painstakingly and lovingly laid for them.

I remain convinced that what we do to and for children during the early years will have a lasting and permanent effect on them and on society. With this in mind, I have written this book to encourage parents and others who have been given the sacred trust of guiding and nurturing African American children.

One of the most important things an elder can give a child is
the gift of time spent with him or her.

Preface:

To the Black Child

HISTORY—1. A statement of what has happened. 2. A systematic, chronological account of important events connected with a country, people, individual, etc., usually with an explanation of causes. 3. A known past. 4. All past events considered together; course of human affairs.

✛

If I speak to you of your history, you will feel great pride. Your history is as old as the earth itself; for history, according to all available scientific proof and anthropological findings, began with the dawn of man on the continent of Africa. And if your true history is to be known, you must become research scholars to unearth the complete and accurate history of your people.

The fact that some people are unwilling to acknowledge the role that Africans have played in the history and achievements of humankind should serve as a catalyst for you to seek unbiased information and the complete truth about African and African American contributions.

As you participate in studying and unearthing the complete history of the human race, you will dispel untruths. In their place you will add to existing knowledge the major role that your family, the African family, has played in this journey down through the ages.

Many attempts have been made to tell world history while excluding your family, but, whenever historians seek truth, clarity and completeness, all roads lead back to your family. Our role as major players in the development of world civilization will be revealed. This, however, does not give you bragging rights, for history in and of itself has little value and few people are willing to learn the lessons that history can teach us. It is only when you are willing to examine history in terms of how it impacts today and tomorrow that it garners meaning.

Mama may have
Papa may have
But God bless the
child that's got
his own.
—*Billie Holiday*

History is a springboard for you to meet the challenges of tomorrow. You are the designers of the future. You must build skyscrapers, find new cures for diseases and continue to explore beyond earth's boundaries. It is you that must help feed the hungry, shelter the homeless and turn the world from war to peace.

Prepare well for your future. The world awaits the contributions and discoveries that only your generation can unveil. This is your challenge.

Preface:

To White Parents and Readers

When I considered the challenge of writing a book about raising children, I wrestled with the idea of writing about children in general. After all, children are children and many of the concerns I address in the book are concerns that all parents have as they try to guide their children in positive ways.

Many common threads run through *The Joy and Challenge* that you will recognize immediately. Parents, both white and African American, love their children. They want what is best for them. Good parents are willing to make sacrifices for their children. Good parents, no matter the race, are protective of their offspring. And forward-thinking parents of all races want their children to inherit a world better than their own.

To whites who take the time to read this book, written from an African American mother/educator's perspective, I believe that you will be enriched and informed in a way that will challenge you to look at the world a little differently and to broaden your perspectives.

Even though our starting points may be different based on culture and environment, the issues that challenge us are the same: All children need acceptance, unconditional love, opportunities to learn, and a safe home and community environment in which to flourish.

With family life across America increasingly under seige by negative forces, we dare not concede the battle. The turmoil and horrific problems that we face will be solved by the joint effort of the races, for the problems that beset us are human problems. The faces of victims of drug addiction, crime and violence, poverty, teen pregnancy and AIDS can be interchanged between the races.

As children see us unite to create a better world, as they see us reach out a hand of friendship, as they see us embrace positive and peaceful attitudes, they will model our behavior; and they, more easily than we, will recognize that all humankind is more alike than different.

While respecting the differences of culture and history, let us unite around our similarities to build a more beautiful world for our rainbow of children.

Red and yellow, black and white and brown, children are precious in God's sight.

Introduction:

From High Adventure to a Stony Road

Evidence suggests that Africans sailed the oceans in search of adventure and to trade with the people of other continents centuries before European explorers mustered the courage to sail to the "edge" of the earth.

One of the places these African adventurers explored would later be known as the Americas. They traded with and lived among the indigenous people and obviously made a lasting impression on them. This is evident in paintings, artifacts and pre-Columbian massive granite carvings found in Mexico and other countries.

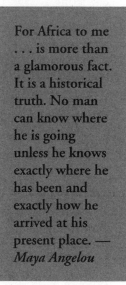

For Africa to me . . . is more than a glamorous fact. It is a historical truth. No man can know where he is going unless he knows exactly where he has been and exactly how he arrived at his present place. — *Maya Angelou*

These African mariners could never have imagined that centuries later their offspring would return to the Americas, not as explorers and traders, but in the bowels of slave ships. Those who were strong enough to survive this horrible crossing of the Atlantic would provide the backbreaking labor needed to build a fledgling group of colonies that would declare its independence from England some one hundred fifty years later. Their "services" would continue to be used for another several centuries as a young nation expanded west, defiling the land with the blood of the native people.

As these enslaved Africans toiled, they harbored dreams of

freedom. Most went to their graves without tasting freedom; yet, they passed the idea of freedom to succeeding generations.

When "freedom" came, they discovered that their condition had improved only slightly as they ventured from the plantation with no severance pay, no possessions, no education and certainly not the promised forty acres and a mule.

They continued to be physically and mentally abused as they moved from pillar to post in search of a place to survive. Their condition improved only slightly as they moved from slavery to a new form of servitude known as sharecropping. After working someone else's land and producing a crop, the landowner would sell the crop and pay the sharecropper a small amount. If the sharecropper lived on the owner's land and bought food and staples from the owner's store, he often found that instead of collecting a wage at harvest time, he was deeply in debt to the landowner. The landowner often used trickery to make sure the sharecropper remained indebted. What could the sharecropper do about this ongoing debt? Usually very little. How were these hardworking sharecroppers able to survive? They had to accept their lot because the laws did not protect them. They endured because they believed that someday their children would enjoy conditions better than their own.

Struggling along with a tremendous weight on their backs in the form of Jim Crow laws, constant abuse, and pittance wages from sharecropping and an assortment of jobs that others would not do, these men, women and children continued to stand tall. But how tall can one stand under the weight of such burdens? How tall can one stand while watching their loved ones and friends tortured and lynched? Lynched for slight offenses or no offenses at all. Lynched for acting saucy or uppity, lynched for quarreling. . . Still there were those who risked life and limb, sometimes losing both, to speak out against these unrelenting atrocities.

These courageous blacks who fought and died on the front lines of every war, who performed backbreaking labor for pennies,

who wetnursed white babies, who migrated north to avoid violence and in search of promise, who suffered every degradation
and humiliation known to mankind, still came up short in a land
that was unwilling to share its blessings and liberties with the sons
and daughters of former slaves.

There was little social and economic change for blacks until
the 1950s gave birth to the civil rights movement. This movement
really should have come as no surprise. Black people had simply
grown tired. They had grown tired individually and collectively of
living day-to-day under dehumanizing conditions. And the day
came, as it always does, when people recognize that a change has
to come. The time for change was ripe—ripened by a long line of
unsung heroes and heroines who never felt comfortable "staying in
their place." People like Nat Turner, Sojourner Truth, Harriet
Tubman, Frederick Douglass, Booker T. Washington, Marcus
Garvey, W.E.B. DuBois, Ida B. Wells, and Mary McLeod Bethune
found dozens of ways to resist a system established to keep them in
line.

The rest of the story is history as Rosa Parks, Martin Luther
King, Jr., Ralph Abernathy, Malcolm X, Fannie Lou Hamer,
Stokely Carmichael and others used their predecessors as starting
blocks for running the race toward freedom, justice and dignity.

During the 1960s, as civil rights were written into laws,
opportunities for blacks increased rapidly. We were beginning to
move into the mainstream. Jobs that had been reserved for "whites
only" were suddenly available. Doors of major colleges and universities opened and enterprising ventures were funded.

Black became beautiful as the great-grandchildren of former
slaves sought a new and more positive racial identity. The effort to
identify with our physical essence took the form of natural hair-
styles and African dress, while other efforts to characterize racial
pride were apparent in a new way of walking, talking, and an
assertiveness in keeping with a growing sense of pride and dignity.

Enter the 1970s and suddenly a door is shut, then another and
another. We were witnessing the beginnings of white backlash.

We were entering a period when many whites felt that blacks had made enough gains. They found a measure of relief in the Supreme Court's 1978 *Bakke* decision on a lawsuit filed by a white man claiming reverse discrimination.

Efforts to undo some four hundred years of trying to stand tall despite a weighted back were no longer grounds for preferential treatment. Gains that had been made began to erode, and opportunities found at the height of the civil rights movement were no longer available.

Throughout the eighties and nineties, benign neglect has continued. The practice of simply ignoring the plight of people on the bottom rung of the social and economic ladder and the refusal of the government to redress past and present discrimination is now seen by many as the right thing to do.

✛

American society has been in an upheaval for the past few decades as old mores were questioned and discarded with little put in their place. This "anything goes" attitude has helped create a climate of crime, violence and disrespect for human life. No citizen can escape the turbulence of life in America today. And while everyone is affected, the problems are greatly exacerbated in African American communities.

Crime and violence are holding many of our communities hostage. Neighborhoods that were once considered safe and stable have become virtual war zones manned by drug dealers, hustlers of human flesh, petty criminals, and gangster types emboldened by easy access to high-powered assault weapons. Drive-by shootings spread death and destruction. Our children are killing each other due to hopelessness, low self-esteem and self-hatred. Some are cashing in their lives for drugs, while others are having their futures short-circuited by lack of a quality education and by early parenthood.

National summits are called, problems discussed, solutions suggested. Local leaders return to their communities determined to do something about the escalating crime and violence in African American communities. Yet, the problems persist and grow worse.

What are the solutions and where are the solutions to these heart-wrenching problems that have become so complex that no one simple approach will work? I believe it will take multiple efforts and approaches, and a great deal of time, to rework negative forces that are firmly entrenched. Not the least of these must be a belief that regaining control of our children through the family will be the real turning point in this nightmare.

✤

If those early African mariners could speak to us, what would they say?

If our ancestors that endured the slave ships and every degradation known to mankind could speak to us, what would they say? And finally, what would their children who experienced emancipation say?

I believe that they would tell us to stop making excuses, to mend our ways, to take back our neighborhoods and rid them of drugs and violence, to rebuild our families, and to restore the dignity that we once had. They would say that we must invest in young people, for without them we have no meaningful future.

They would say, let not their living and dying have been in vain.

SECTION 1

Home and Family

CHAPTER ONE

Yes, Times Have Changed

During the Great Depression, millions of people had one goal in mind—getting enough food to survive until the next day. Jobs and money were scarce items. This economic disaster ravished a still young and growing nation. Yet, the United States survived the Depression and began to rebuild.

As soon as the nation began to recover, World War II captured its attention and resources. The nation survived the war and enjoyed tremendous economic growth in the fifties.

Adults had their share of problems and certainly did not view children as having any significant problems or concerns. Children were instructed to be good, go to school, do schoolwork, do homework, and perform a few chores around the house. Any extra time could be spent doing odd jobs to earn a buck or just hanging out with friends.

> If the house is to be set in order, one cannot begin with the present; he must begin with the past.
> — *John Hope Franklin*

Whether a child completed high school or dropped out, some sort of work could usually be found. If that wasn't exciting enough, young men could enlist in the Army, Navy, Air Force or Marines, while girls improved domestic skills and anticipated marriage and family. If you were one of a lucky few, you could go to college which meant you could delay the pressures of adulthood for a few years.

Was life really ever that simple? Not if you were black and growing up in America. All of the problems during that period of time were magnified if you were a person of African descent living in America. Being born African American carried a stigma that

The child who is read to regularly is given the universe of imagination to explore.

could not be discarded. Little complications became bigger complications, small obstacles to peace and happiness were magnified. Not only did African Americans have to survive during the harshest of economic times, they had to survive in communities and in a nation that as a whole was hostile to their very existence. Yet, survive they did. They raised families and kept inching forward despite Jim Crow laws to keep them "in their places."

Even while surviving and finding their own ways to maintain life, enjoy a few liberties, and seek happiness, few of today's elderly African Americans or those of past generations could have dreamed that their children and grandchildren would face the complex problems that have become commonplace in our neighborhoods and in the nation today.

They never dreamed of the powerful debilitating addiction of crack cocaine.

They never imagined the large numbers of young children having baby after baby without the financial ability to care for them; nor the skirting of responsibility by young men who father children and never look back. Their thoughts would not have been of children having children; of children clearly too young to be able to nurture and give guidance to babies because they lack maturity and are still trying to grow up themselves when parenthood visits.

Nor could they have imagined drive-by shootings. They who had to walk gingerly in society to avoid being thrown in jail for slight or imagined offenses, who tried not to offend or appear to be uppity less they find themselves on the end of a noose could never have dreamed that their children and grandchildren would think life so cheap, so meaningless that they now spill each other's blood—or anyone else's—for offenses as small as feeling that someone looked at them in the wrong way.

They never dreamed of the large numbers of African American males in the penal system. Nor could they have fathomed the street gangs that control neighborhoods, frightening and killing innocent citizens who may have on the wrong color. These gangs are able to lure and recruit our babies and control their lives before they complete elementary school.

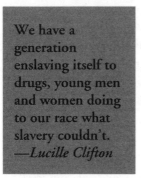

We have a generation enslaving itself to drugs, young men and women doing to our race what slavery couldn't.
—*Lucille Clifton*

A glimpse at the statistical data bears out the dismal news heard morning, noon, and night. The Children's Defense Fund projections on the status of African American children can make one weep. For African American males, one in twenty-four will go to prison, one in forty-five will use cocaine, one in four will drop out of school, one in ten will become a victim of violent crime. But only one in ninety-four will become a teacher, one in 372 a lawyer, one in 684 a physician, and only one in four thousand will earn a Ph.D. in engineering. Of African American females, two out of five will become teenage mothers, one in seven will drop out of high school, one in twenty-one will be a victim of violent crimes, while only one in 356 will become a lawyer, one in 891 a physician and one out of 21,000 will earn a Ph.D. in engineering.

These disheartening projections can change if African American parents and caregivers are willing to launch an intense and concerted effort to reverse these appalling statistics.

We must find ways to protect innocent children from unacceptable negative experiences, such as alcoholism, violence, drug addiction, sexual and physical abuse and mental and physical neglect. For millions who have never known stability and happiness, a way must be found to break the web that entangles them in hopelessness.

We are challenged to find ways to reach out to children who live down to low expectations, who seem to have no value system, who have no thoughts of a bright future, and who have never entertained big dreams.

While thousands of young African Americans from grade school to college have found a way to hold fast to dreams, there are millions who have not. For them life is already the "broken-winged bird that cannot fly" that Langston Hughes wrote of.

Children are not born with broken wings. They are born with young, tender wings that contain all that is needed to fly high. For children to grow strong and spread their wings in wonderful ways, they must be carefully tended by the adults in their lives. If some already have broken wings, it is apparent that the adults in their lives have failed them. Those entrusted with their care, nurturing and guidance have not acted in ways to help them move toward the fulfillment of dreams.

Whose responsibility is it to see that children are encouraged and guided in ways to hold fast to dreams? It is the responsibility of the entire "village." And first and foremost, it is the responsibility of the parents, both male and female. Heads of households

No community institution succeeds without the involvement
of the people of the community.

make the greatest impact and are in a unique position to mold
children in positive ways. When their effort is combined with that
of others in the child's sphere, children soar.

Heads of households should believe and act in ways that
recognize their responsibility, power and influence in determining
the direction and well-being of the family unit. Add the support
and influence of the extended family, educators, other individuals,
community and civic organizations, religious institutions, foun-
dations, and municipal and national government agencies, and
then meaningful change will come about in the lives of children
and the grim statistics will be reversed.

While some strategies will call for dollar investments, the
greater investment will come in terms of quality time, energy and
commitment invested in our sons and daughters.

Most parents, no matter their racial and socio-economic
background, want their children to have a safe and happy child-

hood. They want them to grow into secure, responsible, independent, law-abiding citizens. They have dreams that their children will be more successful than they are and that they will reach their full potential.

African American parents want nothing less for their children. They want their children to learn and laugh and play. If they can shield them from hurt, harm or danger, they will. They want them to feel secure, to be happy, and to enjoy all the fun times that should go along with being a child. Doing well in school is a hope that practically all parents carry for their children.

The lives of our children are too precious to be left to chance. We cannot let them be tossed about by the winds of chance nor let their lives dry up "like raisins in the sun." We must do all within our power to guide them and to salvage those whose names are added to the roll of negative statistics. We must help them realize that life has meaning. At best, life is short. It is meant to be lived fully, productively, and completely.

We must reverse the ill winds to honor the ancestors who realized few dreams for themselves but carried hope for generations yet unborn. We must seize those dreams and make them flourish in our children.

Lost faith in our ability to guide them must be reclaimed. By investing in our children, we save ourselves. We cannot afford to lose our children, ourselves.

CHAPTER TWO

Parental Challenges

The Challenge of Raising Children

Raising children has never been easy. If you are a parent, raising children will probably prove the most difficult and ongoing challenge that you will ever face. It can also prove to be one of life's most enjoyable challenges.

There are several reasons why raising children is extremely challenging. First, no one has yet discovered an exact formula for raising children from infancy to adulthood. We feel our way through many situations that develop as the child grows. Second, most people raise their children in much the same way that they were raised, even failing to change the things in raising their children that they did not like or appreciate in their own upbringing. Third, each child is unique and very special. What works for one child in a given situation may not be the best choice for another child, even within the same family. Finally, you only have one opportunity to raise your children.

> What shall I give my children? who are poor, who are adjudged the leastwise of the land. — Gwendolyn Brooks

It is interesting to observe and hard to understand why some parents seem to put very little effort into childrearing and yet have children that turn out just fine, while other parents may have done everything within their power to give their children a stable and healthy upbringing and yet find a child going down the "wrong" path. Even while observing such paradoxes, parents must do everything within their power to raise their children the very best that they can.

✢

I talked recently with a young couple who had just had their first child. They were ecstatic over the birth of their beautiful nine-pound baby boy. Even though they were excited over becoming three, the new parents were apprehensive at the prospect of raising a baby, especially an African American male, in today's society. Their concerns and fears are real, given the violent and turbulent conditions in our society today that can overwhelm new parents, as well as experienced ones.

Like this young couple, most parents recognize that raising children will be demanding; they just didn't have any idea just how demanding and challenging the job would be.

You didn't really think raising children would be a game of paper dolls and playing house, did you? Of course you didn't. We're talking about real, honest-to-goodness live children. Babies scream and holler at 3:00 a.m., get wet, always seem hungry, and can be temperamental and fretful while you try to figure out what the problem is. Unlike paper dolls, real children cannot be put in dollhouses and forgotten about for days at a time. Unlike paper dolls, real children come in miniature form but grow and grow until they are as big or bigger than you. Along with the physical growth is the growth in their demands for time, guidance, and attention. The excitement and joy of raising real children is coupled with anxiety, challenges that were not anticipated, and ongoing sacrifices.

Joy comes when you watch their cute little antics as they grow. Joy comes when they mimic our movements and babble their first attempts at speech. Joy comes when their sweet cherub faces light up in recognition of you. Joy comes when we hold them close and rock them to sleep.

You feel happy when they celebrate their first birthday and squish their tiny fingers in the cake. You feel happy and relieved when they finally decide that they will use the potty instead of their diaper. Definitely, no paper dolls live here.

As you raise your children, you feel sad at the thought of difficulties that will face them simply because they are children of the sun. At times, you may be overcome with sadness as you realize that others may try to restrict their potential. You feel sadness and a great deal of anxiety when you realize that by the time they reach adolescence, people may fear them when they come face to face on the street. This fear is a blanket fear that engulfs many citizens, not because of any criminal actions on the part of your child, but because too many people see all black children in a negative light. Your feelings of anxiety double when you realize that your child is more likely to be stopped by a law enforcement officer because he is African American, and the reality that his encounter could end in violence or arrest a greater percentage of the time than if he were not African American. We can tape a torn paper doll back together. Not so when our real children are badly torn.

You feel happiness when your child begins school on a positive note. You feel happiness if he is learning at a rapid rate and has a teacher who respects and loves all children. On the other hand, feelings of anxiety sweep over you if your child is not getting off to a good start in school. You feel sad and perhaps angry, too, if you sense that the teacher does not expect much from your son or daughter even before getting to know them.

What does all of this mean? It means raising children of the sun is one big challenge after another. Raising them to adulthood will entail a great deal of sacrifice. No paper dolls live here. These live little people require a great deal of your time and attention.

❖

What makes the job of raising children so difficult? The fact that you do not live on an island alone with just your family—nor would you want to—and the magnitude of the problems we face as a society increase the challenges of child rearing. There is an ongoing media blitz of around-the-clock crime and violence. We hear daily reports of adults and children who are subjected to physical, mental and sexual abuse. Unprecedented numbers of homeless individuals roam our streets, cast aside as just a little bit or a whole lot crazy. The fear of deadly sexually transmitted diseases is paralyzing as new findings reveal that more and more adults, as well as children, have become infected with the HIV virus.

Drug use, both legal and illegal, holds many citizens in a powerful grip. Assault weapons find their way into the hands of children who were just being potty trained nine or ten years ago. Lyrics that call for indecency and promiscuity soar to number one on the music charts. Girls who are still growing and needing to be mothered suddenly find themselves struggling to mother children of their own. Too many boys who lack the guidance of fathers are receiving the distressing news that they are about to become fathers, fathers to children that they are unable to and often unwilling to support.

Each day we drive past schools that are no longer centers of intellectual challenge and havens from the outside world, but instead are corridors of violence where the strong prey upon the weak, where drugs are sold and used on school property, and where students sink their parents into debt so that they can draw the admiration of their peers by dressing in the latest designer fashions. (In addition to drawing admiring looks, these clothes also attract the criminal element who beat, rob and even murder them for their fashionable clothing, athletic shoes and other expensive items.) In this same environment, some African American students who seek to achieve academically find themselves not admired but ridiculed, snubbed or beaten up. They are labeled as oddballs, nerds, and accused of "acting white."

Like it or not, this is real life in the United States today. Whether we realize it, we are all affected by this real-life scenario. You can run but you cannot hide from the mean and ugly side of American life. Hardly a family from Maine to California, and Alaska and Hawaii, too, has not been touched directly or indirectly by violence and crime. Mental anguish and feelings of helplessness grip our entire nation in a huge vise.

Should we throw up our hands and give up or dig our heels in and fight back? Of course we must fight back. Children are too precious to be cast aside and abandoned in their efforts to survive in a world that grows increasingly mad.

Whatever your efforts, and however small they seem, we can make progress. It is the small but united efforts of individuals and individual families that will turn the tide.

Be prepared to encourage though others may discourage. Believe that your encouragement means more than any other person's discouragement, because it does. Be prepared to sacrifice in terms of your total involvement in your child's life. Really get to know your children and seek to understand them. Begin to carry on a daily dialogue with your children while they are very young. This dialogue will lengthen and change as they mature. Be prepared to answer all sorts of questions. Never put off answering a child's question. If she raises a question, she obviously has a concern. Try to give an answer that is appropriate for her age. Also, recognize that some questions do not have easy answers nor immediate answers. Sometimes your answer may be that you do not know the answer. You and your child may wish to seek the answer together.

Expect questions concerning racial matters early in your child's life. Another child at pre-school or kindergarten will point out your child as "different." Be prepared to discuss this "difference" as a positive, not a negative.

Read to your children daily. Take them to the library. Take them to see everything that is appropriate for their age group in your city and in other cities and states. Take the time to go outdoors and play with them. Play games inside, as well. Teach them the games of your childhood. Playing family games promotes family togetherness.

Above all, realize that investing in your child's education will pay big dividends to everyone — the child, the family, African American people, and the nation as a whole. Being an active participant in the education of your child will move him toward fulfilling his potential and gaining future independence. A child that is given a proper education, which includes achieving marketable skills, will not be calling you for financial help at the ages of twenty-five or thirty. As he uses his skills and advanced training, he will not only fulfill his potential but will add to a positive ripple effect that is desperately needed in all African American communities and the nation.

Parents, you are the first and most important ambassadors that your children will ever have. You only have one chance to raise them. How you meet this wonderful challenge is in your hands.

Racism—The Ugly R That Won't Go Away

How do you explain racism to our beautiful innocent children? What can you say to them to make them understand? What can you do to protect them from it? And what can be done to eradicate this ugly position adopted by so many people?

Saying that it is difficult to explain racism to children is an understatement. Yet, we, more than any other people, find ourselves in the position of trying to explain to young and innocent children what racism is and how it works.

We are faced with the unpleasant task of trying to explain racist actions to our young children because racism shows up early in the lives of most African Americans. It is unwanted, unwelcomed and not expected, but it always shows up. Whether on the job, at school, in the neighborhood, in the rhetoric of politicians, from a playmate or "friend," or while walking or driving down the street, it keeps coming at you.

Explaining to today's children what is happening is made even more difficult by the fact that the old racist tactics often have on a new suit. Modern racism is often refined and smiling and may appear harmless at first, but if you have lived a while and you are black in America, the ability to recognize racism becomes second nature. Even when you are not looking for it and are feeling relaxed and at peace with the world, it comes looking for you.

Many of the negative racial attitudes can be traced back to our entry into this country. Unlike many ethnic Americans, we did not enter standing on the deck of a ship gazing longingly at France's gift of the Statue of Liberty. In fact, we came long before Lady Liberty was in place. Even if she had been there, we would not have seen the inscription from Emma Lazarus's poem, "Bring me your tired, your weary, your huddled masses yearning to breathe free," for there is no view for those chained and shackled in the belly of a slave ship. We did not reach this country knowing that we would become eligible for full citizenship after a few years. No, the Constitution of the United States defined us as only three-fifths of a person.

The circumstances of our arrival seemed to negate any possibility of being thought of as full and equal human beings to those who brought us here. So from the very beginning of our tenure on American soil, it has been an uphill battle to attain rights and privileges that others are able to take for granted.

Because racism has been around a very long time and has made its way into the institutions of our society, it is often seen as the natural order. It has become so legitimized that even its victims cannot always recognize it for what it is. Some victims unwittingly employ institutionalized racist tactics against their own people. Because certain practices have become so firmly entrenched in the system and are not overt and obviously hostile, many people are unable to recognize systemic racism.

Racism manifests itself in the way many people speak. They always refer to people of a different racial or ethnic background as *the black* doctor, *the Hispanic* cop, *the Asian* teacher. Such references usually add no additional meaning to the sentence except to point out that the person being spoken of is of a different race than the one doing the speaking.

Interestingly, whites are often surprised to learn that blacks find such expressions to be offensive. Blacks, on the other hand, are often just as surprised to learn that whites may be saying such things without any conscious intent. Whites often deny that some of the situations I describe here exist, or if they did exist at one time that they continue today. On the other hand, blacks sometimes have a hard time recognizing that every bad thing that happens to them is not directly caused by racism. As the Alabama sharecropper Nate Shaw declared in the book about him by Theodore Rosengarten, "All God's dangers ain't a white man."

And, since I am speaking frankly about the issue of race in America, I must acknowledge that racism and discrimination injure other minorities, too. Racism also injures the person doing the discriminating and it harms the nation as a whole. In this book, I am addressing the specific problem of how racism affects African American children and how it especially challenges their parents in the raising of these children. I am certainly not suggesting that the Ugly R does not affect Native Americans, Latinos, Asians, or other minorities. Nor am I suggesting that whites are the only ones capable of racist thought or action. But I do believe that because blacks are the largest minority group in the U.S., and because of the special historical and cultural circumstances of slavery and legalized segregation, the problem of racism manifests itself most strongly and is most persistent against blacks.

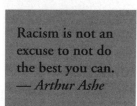

Racism is not an excuse to not do the best you can.
— *Arthur Ashe*

The Ugly R is rampant in our educational system through the tracking of students based on race and economic status. Who says an economically deprived child can't be smart or gifted? Who says African American children cannot be brilliant? But many do feel this way, and unfortunately many educators hold identical views. They feel that low economic status and low intellect are one and the same. Some of these same teachers—both black and white—assume that African American students are not quite as bright as white students and therefore should be steered away from academically challenging subjects.

Examples of this negative attitude are seen when African American students find themselves being admonished by high school counselors that higher level courses may prove too difficult for them.

Racism is obvious when an audience registers shock that a valedictorian is African American. But then again, maybe the announcement of a black valedictorian should provoke surprise since negative forces within many school systems work to ensure that few valedictorians will be African American no matter the student's genius or academic standing. Too often something "comes up" at the last minute to keep a deserving African American child from that place of honor on graduation day.

These assumptions and attitudes are alive and well on university campuses as well. "Advisors" caution African American students to steer clear of certain majors that are considered "too difficult."

Do not sit idly by and watch while others, who do not always have your child's interest at heart, limit her future. Demand that your child be placed in academically challenging courses and continuously monitor her progress. No group has a lock on intelligence. Giftedness and brilliance are found among all ethnic groups.

> Can't nothing make your life work if you ain't the architect. — *Terry McMillan*

If our survival in this nation and contributions to its growth and development mean anything, it is an indication that African American children have substantial intellect and their share of genius that must be recognized and developed.

The Ugly R is present in curriculum content that emphasizes the contributions and lifestyles of the majority group, thus implying that one group is superior to all others. It manifests itself in thousands of classrooms each day when teachers have low expectations of students of color. And when students live down to those expectations, it is seen as acceptable to underachieve. Racism scores another victory when an African American excels academically and is pointed out as exceptional.

Sadly, the Ugly R is fueled within the black race by individuals who can only see the negatives about other black people. They cannot see any of the good that average hard-working, law-abiding citizens are doing. Nor can they see the strengths and talents of black people that are visible everyday. These individuals with low self-concepts have turned on their own in a senseless way. They are our own worst enemies as they try to pass along their low opinions of African Americans to their children. Unfortunately, they are successful much of the time.

We must not remain silent when we hear other blacks attacking the race based on their own brand of self-inflicted racism and without just cause. On the other hand, we must learn to speak out against African Americans who are negative forces. We should band together to force them to clean up their acts. We must never defend blacks whose actions are immoral, self-serving, and injurious to our progress.

Examine your personal views toward other African Americans. You do yourself, your children and the black community no favor by upholding the negative elements in our communities. Whether politicians, teachers, physicians, lawyers, or heads of African American institutions, they must be held accountable for poor or dishonest leadership in a position of trust.

Racism is keeping our nation from becoming all that it can be. We cannot remain a world leader if we do not find solutions to expunge this awful chancre from our midst.

Certain events of the past few years have made it clear that blacks and whites are miles apart in their views of the United States. The president of the United States has been forced to address the issue of the Ugly R. He has called for "cleaning our house of racism."

Our children deserve our best efforts. We cannot afford to become battle-weary when the future for all children is at risk. Children in general need to be taught that the only cure for racism occurs when an individual recognizes that his attitudes and actions are racist, and he desires to change. In the mean time, *your* children need to focus on what they can control—their own achievements and happiness.

Work toward racial understanding and harmony. We cannot

waste time pointing fingers, for that will only lead to denials by those most guilty of such practices. This bantering back and forth will keep us on a treadmill. Individual citizens should engage in dialogue to promote racial understanding and harmony. If we refuse, problems will continue to grow and will become our children's problems to solve.

Discuss racial concerns with your child. Talk in terms of possibilities, not impossibilities. Refuse to carry hatred toward people of other ethnic groups. Instead, use your energy to build bridges of understanding, along with better communities for all of our children to inherit.

CHAPTER THREE

Parental Practices

Affirming Our Children

All human beings need to be loved and affirmed. When a person is affirmed, he feels valued. All human beings need to belong and to feel attached to others. The family, along with an inner circle of friends, serves to enhance our feelings of being valued and loved.

Feeling accepted by those around us is fundamental to our well-being. And this feeling of being valued, accepted, loved and, thereby affirmed, is critically important in the overall development of children.

Parents have a responsibility to affirm their children. The process of affirming children can prove relatively simple, yet difficult at the same time. Simple ways to affirm children are suggested in this book. The difficulty of affirming children comes from the complexity of our society. The United States is in upheaval as we struggle with complex issues of race, class, morality and economics. These issues affect us individually and collectively. They impact our interactions with each other and with our children, making it even more critical that we affirm, time and time again, African American children. Many of the issues being debated in Congress have to do with whether the educational and economic needs of children will be met. Such organizations as the Children's Defense Fund are working tirelessly to save appropriations that, if cut, will have devastating effects on millions of children.

But regardless of what government does, parents must redouble their efforts. When you look at the big picture, can you afford not to affirm your children? The process of affirming them is ongoing and requires deep commitment, time, energy and patience. We must foster a level of self-esteem and self-sufficiency in our children that will enable them to beat the odds that predict they cannot make it.

Those entrusted with the guidance of the young must use affirming practices that serve as springboards to success. It is crucial to recognize that to affirm children, adults must affirm themselves. You cannot bring children along positively if you do not have positive feelings about your own "self." As you affirm yourself, you are better able to accept, value and affirm your children.

Affirming African American children will lead them away from failure and toward a growing number of success stories.

First, Give Them Love

Affirm your child with love. The great Tina Turner sings, *What's love got to do with it?* And the answer is: Everything.

All people respond to words of affection sincerely spoken. And certainly the young, impressionable minds of children will soak up and thrive on verbal affirmations of love.

How many adults have anguished over the fact that, while growing up, their parents never told them that they were loved and gave out few words of praise. These adults may confess that their parents showed acts of love by sheltering, feeding and caring for them, but they still wish their mothers and fathers had found the words to express those feelings.

Perhaps you're not the affectionate type, or you're not much on words. Well, maybe it's time for you to learn. Every beginning, every new behavior has a starting point. So start now. Tell your child that you love him. There need not be a special occasion such as a birthday. Just simply say to the child, "I love you, _____." This can be followed by positive comments such as, "I'm really glad that you are my son/daughter." Verbalizing your feelings may be difficult or seem awkward at first, but the more often that you use terms of endearment, the easier and more natural it will become. Watch your child's face light up as you not only show your love, but verbalize positive emotions as well.

Children will carry these positive messages in their minds to school each day. These messages will play back while in class and bolster their efforts to achieve academically. These messages will play back when peer pressure encourages them to make a wrong move. These messages will play back when those in authority try to convince them subtly or not so subtly that they are worth less than others. They will be propelled by the positive messages that you planted in them. Their faith in themselves and in the knowledge of your love will energize and move them forward.

> I leave you love. Love builds. It is positive and helpful. — *Mary McLeod Bethune*

Make sure that your children know that you love them unconditionally. Love should not be tied to how well they are doing academically nor to how athletically talented they are. It should not be tied to anything. Your sons and daughters should be loved simply because they are your children.

Don't Just Tell Me—Show Me!

Now that you are using the words, let's move into an action mode. Children need to see love demonstrated. Words are not enough. Most of us have had experiences with people who claim to respect us, care about us and love us, but their actions run contrary to their words. A combination of words and actions lets children know that they are valued and loved.

How do you turn words into actions? You can start by centering on your child's good qualities. Every child can do something well. Whatever children do well should be praised. If they are good at sharing, tell them. If they strive to be honest, let them know you are aware of that fine quality. If they strive to excel academically, never take it for granted but continue to praise their efforts. If they make a conscientious effort to keep their room neat and clean, let them know that you are pleased.

Contrary to a widely held belief, praising children will not ruin them, make them vain, or give them the big head. Praising their honest efforts will help develop strong feelings of self-worth that are not easily torn down by negative forces.

How African Americans See Themselves

Because of our history of enslavement, it has been deeply ingrained in many African American people that unless our physical characteristics and features closely resemble people of European descent, then we are unattractive or ugly.

Many blacks can remember a time not long ago when beauty queens and kings from elementary school through college were chosen, not for having good character or other positive qualities, but because these students looked more white than most other blacks. The greater the similarity to European looks, the greater the likelihood that an individual would be chosen to represent a school or some other organization.

In recent years there has been a movement away from such shallow thinking as many African Americans have reassessed their standards of beauty. This movement to recognize our own beauty took root in the sixties with "Black is Beautiful." It has fluctuated, but still seems to be alive and well and can be seen in the selection process of today's beauty queens. The extreme emphasis on European physical traits such as hair texture, skin complexion, facial features, and even body structure has caused a great deal of pain for African American girls growing up in America. In our unwitting efforts to make ourselves over into pseudo-Europeans, we missed the awareness of our own natural beauty.

If we do not seek ways to appreciate the beauty of African American people with complexions ranging from blue-black to high yellow and with a wide range of facial features and hair textures, then we will continue to pass along to each succeeding generation the negatives that impede our feelings of self-worth, well-being and, in many cases, our progress.

Many African American children have no idea of their own beauty because they have had only one standard of beauty held in front of them. That standard dominates the daily images that children see, from television, movies, and magazines to what is said by individuals who hold one-dimensional ideas of beauty.

It is time to see your African American children as the beautiful human beings that they are. Do not continue to hold them to assumed standards of beauty that reflect neither their heritage nor gene pool.

Watching African American adults poke fun at African American features is sending a very damaging and negative message to children of the sun. What is the importance of such matters when men have been to the moon, hearts are transplanted daily, and the need to save the planet looms on the agenda?

Rethinking distorted and one-dimensional attitudes about beauty not only will enhance your child's image of himself, but will also improve your own image of your "self."

Pause today and tell your children that they look good. Make it a point today to tell an African American child that she is pretty, beautiful, a doll. Watch the glow on her face. This positive stroking will result in greater confidence, a stronger self-concept, and feelings of well-being. Children who feel good about themselves are more likely to reach out to others than to strike out at others.

Pretty Is As Pretty Does

On the other hand, avoid giving too much attention to what you may consider positive physical traits. It is good to acknowledge physical beauty, but guard against an overemphasis on such qualities. If you have what you consider a "good-looking" child, this should not become an obsession with you or the child.

We've all seen people who are considered pretty or handsome, but no one can stand being around them because they are so smitten with themselves. Viewing such a self-centered person positively is difficult because it is hard to see beyond their self-centeredness or other ugly personality traits. On the other hand, most of us know people who "aren't much to look at" but they have such winning personalities and exude such strength and love that we never notice that they aren't physically attractive.

> You are beautiful; but learn to work, for you cannot eat your beauty.
> — *Congolese proverb*

While good looks may prove an asset, they will not carry you through life. A person may land a job by cashing in on good looks, but keeping that job may prove quite a different story.

I See You and I Follow You

Have you ever watched a little boy step into his father's shoes, take a few steps and stumble? Little girls like dressing up in mother's old clothes and high heels and putting on makeup. What they are doing besides giving us a chuckle is letting us know how much they want to be like us when they grow up.

What a golden opportunity to shape good character and to develop good habits in our children during the formative years. Good habits are best learned by watching positive role models. Likewise, bad habits are learned from watching role models with bad habits. It is interesting that bad habits take such little effort and are so easily learned. Once learned, they are the hardest to break.

Babies watch and listen intently to adults around them. A baby coos in response to the human voice. If you "pat-a-cake," so will the baby. Mental and physical growth are accelerated during the first few years of life. Because young children watch and imitate, parents have the greatest opportunity to influence and teach good habits by modeling the desired behavior.

What about your habits? Think about your good habits that you would like your child to model. Now think about your bad habits that you hope they do not model or notice.

What about your television viewing habits? Do you view

selectively or do you spend hours watching pathological displays of human behavior, then fuss at the children when they sit wide-eyed and blank-faced looking at television all evening instead of doing chores, homework, reading, practicing a musical instrument, interacting with other family members, or being physically active? Do you spend hours on the telephone gossiping or just chatting about nothing? Do your children ever see you reading a book or magazine? Do you have any worthwhile hobbies that bring personal satisfaction? Have you learned anything new lately?

If you cuss, more than likely your children will outcuss you. If you smoke, there is a strong chance that your children will "light up" at a fairly young age, though this is one habit that may not be passed along as easily because of growing public awareness of the dangers of smoking. If you hit the bottle now and then or if you are a heavy drinker who heads for the liquor cabinet as soon as you come in the door, your child may do the same. If you are worried that the drug elements in the street may infect your child, don't

Teachers are important, but remember that parents are the first and most important teachers.

help them move in that direction by depending on pills, a snort, or a needle to help you solve your problems. If you have a bad habit that you can't break alone, get help for it.

Parents are the first teachers and remain the most important teachers. Telling your children to do as you say and not as you do only confuses them, breeds resentment, drives a wedge between you and your children, and paints an accurate picture of you as a hypocrite. Be an example that your children can follow. Good examples lead them toward self-fulfillment.

> The situation of our youth is not mysterious. Children have never been very good at listening to their elders, but they have never failed to imitate them. — *James Baldwin*

Children see what you do and learn from your habits. Some parents think that their children are too young to know what adults are doing. Not so. Children are very aware and sensitive to their surroundings and learn very quickly. They watch everything that adults do. They remember specific smells, sounds, and actions. As they mature, they are able to put the pieces of the puzzle together. Not only do children learn quickly by modeling adult behavior, but they often have the capacity to carry that behavior to the next level. Whatever you do, they can outdo you given time.

Sibling Equality

If you have at least two children, then sibling equality can become a major concern.

Loving your children equally and practicing sibling equality does not mean that all situations can be handled the same. If all things were equal, you would simply have a clone of your firstborn child. You would also miss the excitement and adventure that come from the differences in your children. If you have more than one child, then you know that no two are alike. Each child must be dealt with as an individual. Children respond differently to a similar set of circumstances, therefore, you must consider the personality of the child in any given situation.

You must consider the child's constitution. Children are seldom all one way or another; they have complex personalities. Some children are timid, others bold; some predictable, others mischievous; some serious, others playful; some quiet, others talkative; some easy going, others high-strung; and some prefer solitude while others are gregarious.

Recognize early on to accept a child's basic personality. Do not make the child miserable and keep yourself upset by trying to remake her. Avoid comparisons of one child to the other.

Do not try to predetermine how to handle situations before they arise. You will need to consider the child and the situation at hand, then determine a course of action. Most children have a strong sense of fairness, even when similar situations are handled differently.

As you strive to be fair and to respond to your children based on their unique personalities, be aware that outsiders are capable of creating dissension and conflict between them by comparing and favoring one over another. Sure, someone may be more attached to one of your children for any number of reasons. However, they should not be allowed to make negative comparisons between the children nor to continually dote over one while ignoring the others. This is not to say that a child who deserves recognition should not get it. The key word is balance.

When working through any situation remember that each child is an individual and must be treated as such. Use common sense and also try placing yourself in the child's shoes. These three factors will help you act wisely as you love, nurture and guide your children.

Are You a Parent or a Buddy?

Some parents create difficulties in the relationship with their children because they have adopted the role of buddy rather than parent. Children need buddies their own ages, but they need parents who are willing to act as guides and help steer them through childhood, adolescence, and into adulthood.

Some parents prefer to be their children's buddies rather than assume their proper role as adult role models. There are many reasons why some parents suffer from role confusion. Some people became parents too early and never had a chance to complete their own teenage stages of growth and development that lead to adulthood. Others refuse to acknowledge that with each passing day, they are, indeed, a day older, then a month older, and then years older. They are afraid to grow older. They believe that by hanging out with their children, they can somehow slow down the clock. Then there are the parents who fear alienation from and rejection by their children if they assume the role of authority figure and disciplinarian.

Someone has to guide the children and correct them, when necessary. If you refuse to give them proper direction, then they will get direction from other sources, sources that you may regret later.

Children need good parents to nurture and guide them. If you are willing to give them the love, protection and guidance that they need, you are assuming a proper and God-given role, and you will be the best friend that your child will ever have.

Discipline as an Act of Love

One of the most difficult challenges of child rearing is learning effective ways to discipline your children.

People will give you all kinds of advice, some of it good and some ridiculous. Some suggestions may seem silly and others cruel. Ultimately you have to decide how to meet the challenge of disciplining your child.

NEGATIVE DISCIPLINE SIGNALS. Let's get a few negatives out of the way first. A sure way to have problems with your child is to be neglectful and ignore him. Some parents are guilty of giving their children material possessions, but seldom give of themselves. Giving of yourself means spending precious time with

Loving discipline leads to well-adjusted children.

your children talking together, working together, studying, playing, or whiling away some time. Children that are neglected will prove difficult to control.

Another way to guarantee problems is to be extremely critical of your child. Criticize everything they do. Make jokes and laugh at his failed attempts to immediately master new things. A child must have time to grow and develop. Keep your expectations in line with his age and abilities. Constant nit-picking and fault finding will cause him to feel mistreated and unloved. He will lack confidence in himself and others, and may soon begin to exhibit negative behaviors.

Overindulging your child is a serious breach of common sense. Overindulgence will lead to self-centeredness. Children don't need this type of spoiling. They do not need everything that they ask for. They do not need to always be "first" in every activity in which they are involved. Start early to teach children how to reach outside of themselves and do for others. They can be taught early that there is a great deal of joy in sharing of one's time, attention, and possessions with others. They also need chores that are appropriate for their age and development. Performing chores teaches responsibility, as well as common ownership of the home.

The most blatant offense that some parents make that insures that their child will be heading for difficulties in the future is to believe that he can do no wrong. Believe everything he says. Always believe everyone else is picking on him. To insure conflict and problems in school talk openly in front of him about how the teacher had better not correct him. Blame every other child for any difficulty that he has with his peers.

POSITIVE DISCIPLINE. Children learn more about how to live and what to do and what not to do from watching parents. They learn to model us by observing everything that we say and do. If you argue and scream at others, they may do the same. If you have a loving, gentle nature, chances are they will also. Whatever you do, watch your child and you will observe your own actions in your child.

Begin to try to reason with your sons and daughters at an early age and in a way that they can understand. Talking out problems and concerns will help them learn how to make better choices. Try this approach versus screaming and hollering and grabbing a belt and whipping them.

When children misbehave or break the rules of the family, seize this opportunity to teach. It is important to talk to them and explain why their behavior is not acceptable and what might have been more appropriate. These discussions will lead to the highest form of discipline which is self-discipline. It is called intrinsic discipline because it comes from within the person. It is their ability to control their own behavior. Everyone should strive for a high level of intrinsic discipline.

Give a child a chance to explain his side of what happened and why. You will learn to see how he thinks, even if you don't agree with him. But remember that you have the final word. Wise parents lead and guide their children, not the other way around.

It takes children quite a while to develop a conscience, a sense of right and wrong. A strong and healthy conscience will develop as the family works in partnership with the school, religious and community institutions. Children that are neglected or mistreated may not develop a strong conscience. They may feel the need to be cunning and deceitful in order to survive and escape punishments that are too severe.

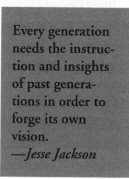

Every generation needs the instruction and insights of past generations in order to forge its own vision.
—*Jesse Jackson*

When you correct your son or daughter, try to keep in control of your emotions. Try not to "go off" on them. This is easier said than done, but try anyway. Though children need correction, they also need understanding and compassion. Sometimes they need to be given a second chance. Allowing for mistakes is important so that he can feel that he has a chance to improve without always having the threat of physical or verbal punishment or the loss of privileges.

Whatever methods of discipline you choose, make sure that they are administered with love and respect. Children that feel loved and respected are more accepting of discipline than those that feel unloved and neglected.

Expose Children to the World Around Them

Though the ability to read well is fundamental to school success, children should experience other important activities to enhance their mental and intellectual growth and development.

Children need multiple and varied experiences that must come from exposure to more than their local neighborhoods. They need to understand early that the world is a much larger place than their "hood." They must be given the opportunity to explore their town or city, then see other regions of the country if at all possible.

Can you afford not to expose your children to more than the local neighborhood? By exposing children to people who look and live differently from them, you are beginning early lessons in not only tolerance, but acceptance and pleasure that can come from diversity. Children find the differences in people and cultures interesting and exciting. How dull if you are always totally surrounded by people who mirror you. How much better off society would be if all parents made an effort to expose their children to people of different cultures, races and creeds. Many of the race-related problems we are having today stem from a lack of knowledge and understanding of people of a different race.

> He who does not travel will not know the value of men. —
> *Berber proverb*

Limited finances need not limit your children's exposure to a bigger world. Children can be involved in many activities that cost little. Take them to the zoo, aquarium, and museums. Many cities now have children's museums. When the circus comes to town, go and enjoy the clowns and animals. Visit a park on the other side of town. Pack a lunch, take books and games, and spend the day in the park. Many farms offer tours of their facilities. [See resources.]

Call the visitors' bureau in your city to find out about points of interest locally and in surrounding areas. Then turn off the television and head out to explore your city several times during the school year and more often during the summer months.

Many of the fun places to visit have free or inexpensive admission. Think of other ways to spend precious time with your children. Make a list of things you would like to do together and place the list on the refrigerator door.

❖

Maybe you are wondering how you can afford a family vacation when money is tight and the economy seems unstable.

You can afford a family vacation by planning your trip well in advance and saving for it. If you have difficulty establishing a separate vacation savings account, then charge it. Most people are charging everything else these days, much of which is impulse

Children never forget what they learn on a family trip.

buying. They are burdened down with installment payments and cannot even remember what was purchased. Many items are worn out or broken down before they are paid off. While charging a vacation may not be the very best way to pay for a trip, it will be money well spent.

Convince yourself that your family needs and deserves an annual vacation. If there is no way you can take a vacation every year, then shoot for every other year. It need not be an expensive trip to some faraway fantasy island or elaborate resort. It may be within a few hours drive of your home, but a getaway is a getaway and will prove rejuvenating and a learning experience for the entire family.

Visiting historic places is one way to make books come alive. Every child should be taken on a trip to our nation's capitol, Washington, D.C. The family should also visit some of the growing number of African American historic sites. [See resources.]

Many parents dress their children in designer outfits and expensive athletic shoes. They support their children's music listening habits by purchasing the latest compact disks and tapes, yet claim poverty when it comes to spending money on a family outing or vacation. It's really a matter of priorities. By traveling with your child, you are showing that you understand the importance of investing in his future by exposing him to a world larger than his local neighborhood. African American children need this opportunity so that they will be able to compete with other children in the world community.

CHAPTER FOUR

Acceptance and Expectations

The most important thing that you can do for your child is to accept him for who he is. Acceptance means understanding that he is an individual. He is an unique creation. Accept everything about him that he has no control over. Accept his physical appearance, his left or right handedness. If he's short or tall, fat or skinny, accept him. Whatever the human form, be accepting because human beings come in all forms, sizes, shapes and with varying degrees of ability in many areas.

Most of us would change something about ourselves if we could. As mentioned earlier, besides the usual run-of-the-mill things that most people would change, too many African Americans carry extra and needless burdens about our appearance.

Though the movement of the sixties with its "Black is Beautiful" phrase pointed us in the right direction, this positive emphasis did not go far enough to remove deeply imbedded centuries old feelings of inferiority. Many of us still see ourselves as too black, our features as too full and our hair as too kinky.

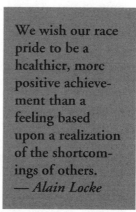

We wish our race pride to be a healthier, more positive achievement than a feeling based upon a realization of the shortcomings of others.
— *Alain Locke*

If these negatives are all you've ever heard applied to your own people, then it is difficult to overcome them, but not impossible. Decide to raise yourself to a higher level of racial consciousness and appreciation by working hard to overcome the in-race prejudices that are prevalent and damaging. Make a conscious effort not to pass this twisted mentality to your children. The very next time you are inclined to think negatively about your own people in terms of hair, skin color, features and body structure, pause and ask why you have that particular attitude.

Perhaps you cannot change the way a large percentage of black people see themselves, but you can exercise control over your own thinking. You can learn to love yourself as you are and you can teach your children to do the same.

> You are young, gifted and black. We must begin to tell our young, there's a world waiting for you, yours is the quest that's just begun.
> — *James Weldon Johnson*

One of the best gifts that a parent can give a child is unconditional acceptance. Though others in a society may have less than legitimate reasons for not accepting your child, she should not have to deal with lack of acceptance from you. When children are loved and accepted within the family unit for who they are, there is less chance that negative influences outside the home will have as strong an impact on them.

Accept yourself and accept your African American child for all that she is and for all the potential that she will realize given the opportunity. The refined, intelligent, productive woman is in the girl. The self-assured, intelligent, productive man is in the boy.

Along with this high level of acceptance should come a high level of expectation. Expect your child to do well. Expect her to achieve. Expect her to be a decent human being and considerate of others.

There is a saying, "I never expect much out of life, and so far I haven't been disappointed." This is meant to draw laughter for a do-nothing, expect-nothing attitude that too many people have. But the sad side of this little joke is that it is a self-fulfilling prophecy. If you expect little, you get little or maybe nothing at all. On the contrary, if your actions reflect high expectations, more than likely you will achieve at a higher level than someone with low expectations.

What message do you send your children? Expect a great deal from them and they will rise to the occasion. Expecting high achievement and success from your children is another way of showing them that you believe in them. They will know that they are valued and loved.

Everyone needs a challenge. If there are no expectations, then there is no challenge. Just as we challenge our children to grow strong and healthy by eating properly and exercising through play

Encourage your children to accept challenges and set goals.

and sports, we should challenge them intellectually by holding up high expectations and creating a climate in which they can flourish and achieve those expectations.

Once children learn to set high expectations, they will carry this habit into adulthood. Whatever they are involved in, encourage them to do their best. That is the way to teach them to play to win. Playing to win is not always coming in first in a contest, but setting high expectations for oneself and then giving it your best efforts in order to fulfill those expectations. Winning is putting everything into the game.

Children must be taught to set goals that are challenging. What good is accomplished if a goal is set below capabilities? On a scale of one to ten, his aim should always be toward the top of the scale. If he is consistently shooting for a five or below, where's the challenge? Encourage him to aim high. Then if he falls a little short, maybe he will land at eight or nine instead of one or two.

Whether it is academic achievement, athletic prowess, school

A child who spends time with other high achievers will raise his own standards and performance.

extracurricular activities such as drama class, or mastery of a musical instrument, help your child understand that the return will be based on the effort expended. And remember that whatever the level of achievement, praise your child's effort.

Failure comes easily and requires little output. On the other hand, accomplishment requires hard work and determination. If failure comes, as it does from time to time, let it not be from lack of effort. We must understand and help our children understand that the greatest failure is failing oneself.

> One does not become great by claiming greatness.
> — *Xhosa people of South Africa*

When expectations are met, when the hard work is done and the successes follow, the crowd of supporters swells. Remember, everyone loves a winner, and winning means putting everything into the game.

CHAPTER FIVE

Attitudes and Actions

Empowering Your Child to Dream Big Dreams

The most effective way to teach your child to dream big dreams is to let them observe you dreaming big dreams.

The quickest way to kill a dream is to share it with people who have none. Hang around with people who have no dreams and ambitions and they will destroy yours. Some of the dullest and most uninteresting people in life, who practically vegetate day-to-day, become negatively animated when you mention a dream or ambition that you have. Such people have no particular aspirations and cannot understand why you do. Because they lack aspirations, they seem programmed to attack your dreams.

Too many African Americans have mental roadblocks to dreaming. Avoid people who have established mental roadblocks for themselves because they will intentionally and unintentionally set up mental roadblocks for you.

Some of our mental roadblocks are as weak as "I'm too old to do this or that." "I don't have a way to get from point A to point B." "I'm exhausted!" These mental roadblocks are grounded in a period of time not long ago when we were told that we were nothing and could accomplish little. When an African American did accomplish great things, too many people were quick to point out that individual an exception. We often fail to realize that some people achieve because they brush aside mental roadblocks and move straight ahead to accomplish goals that they have set for themselves.

Although these negative mental attitudes should have been buried generations ago, they are alive and well and thriving among people that can least afford such attitudes—African Americans. Some of the worst negative mental roadblocks are given new life daily. They can be seen in the actions of too many black people who act out their self doubts and self-hatred. These roadblocks are given fresh life daily as negative beliefs spill from the lips of African Americans who have little faith in themselves and their people. The saddest part of this scenario is that it is played out in front of young minds. Children listen to everything that adults say and give weight to such negative statements.

Listed are examples of the type of negative statements that children and adults are subjected to on any given day, followed by possible counters. Try not to counter in a brash way, but speak to the issue in a matter-of-fact manner. What you want is to raise someone's consciousness. You want them to really think and explore their own attitudes and feelings, not put them on the defensive.

NEGATIVE: You just can't do business with black people. I'm never going back there because . . .

COUNTER: Why not talk with the management to try to resolve the problem? Don't just turn away in a huff intent on putting out the word against this business. Do you stay away from a white-run establishment because of bad service? Most of us return to that business establishment time and time again even though the service that they offer may not be the best. Many of us grumble to a friend, then return to that same business when a sale is advertised. You should lodge a formal complaint with any business whenever you are dissatisfied.

NEGATIVE: Never go to a black lawyer or doctor.

COUNTER: Why not? There are unscrupulous, incompetent, and unethical white lawyers and doctors. Surely you don't think lawyers have earned a bad name because of the handful of black ones. Would you rather go to a white doctor who ranked at the bottom of his class than a black doctor at the top of his class?

When you run into negative, unscrupulous, or poorly trained professionals, try to deal with them individually instead of castigating every African American in that profession. Do you want someone to judge your capabilities based on your skin color or race?

NEGATIVE: "They" aren't going to give you a promotion. You've gone as far as "they" will let you go.

COUNTER: Be more specific. Who is "they" and who's going to stop me from moving ahead? "They" do not have the final say on my ultimate success. When I decide that I have gone as far as I can go in this organization, it will be my decision to move on. Besides, I've gained some experience here and I can use that experience to start my own business where there is no glass ceiling.

These type attitudes speak to a lack of belief in one's self and one's people. They are very easily transferred to large numbers of black children who too often struggle with feelings of inadequacy and self-doubt.

Check your thinking for mental roadblocks. Do you hear yourself in any of the above statements? If so, you are your own and your child's worst enemy. You have set limitations for yourself by your way of looking at the world. When you learn to look at all people as individuals with talents, aspirations and capabilities, you will no longer place glass ceilings over their heads, over your own head and over the heads of your children. Breaking the cycle of self-doubt begins with you.

Dreamkillers

People who have no dreams and are loaded with mental roadblocks have to be busy doing something, so they spend a considerable amount of time discussing the impracticality or foolishness of your dreams. Show me a person who shoots down your dreams before you can get them out of your mouth and I'll show you someone who doesn't know how to dream and certainly doesn't have any dreams of his own. This person is almost always afraid to take risks. If they ever had a dream and it did not become a reality, they threw in the towel long ago. Dreaming requires risks. Talk to anyone who has envisioned a dream, set a goal, and turned it into a reality and you will find that the path they chose was anything but risk-free.

African American history is replete with success stories of people who started out with little more than the tattered shirts on their backs and dreams in their hearts. We have Harriet Tubman, who dreamed of freedom, but didn't stop with her own; Thurgood Marshall, who reached the highest court in the land, the Supreme Court. His career as a lawyer fighting for the rights of black and poor people shaped his tenure on the bench where his decisions protected those who are underrepresented as a matter of

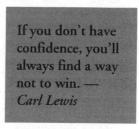

If you don't have confidence, you'll always find a way not to win. — *Carl Lewis*

course. Today there are bright young women like Mae Jemison, who envisioned being an astronaut. She became the first African American female to rocket into outer space. Stop for a moment and look around you. There are hundreds of success stories visible to you within your own community. These individuals contribute to the growth and vitality of their communities and the nation.

❖

What dreams do you have? Whether you dream of returning to school after years away from a classroom, building your dream house, starting a business, changing careers, improving your physical appearance by shedding extra pounds, or acquiring new skills that will make you more marketable, you can be certain that some "friends" are waiting in the wings to tell you why your dream will not work. If you allow them, they will convince you that you are wasting your time and how foolish you are to try. These are the people who are armed and extremely dangerous. One thing is certain: If you continue to spend time with them, you will soon put your dreams and ambitions on hold. You will soon be doing the same thing that your "friends" are doing—nothing! In fact, after a while you will forget that you ever had dreams.

Perhaps you have a "dreamless" friend and you really like this person and you've known him a long time and do not wish to appear unloyal. The choice is yours. You have much to lose by continuing to hang around with this dead weight. Trying to convince others of the legitimacy of your projects and dreams is a waste of time and energy. They cannot be convinced. Furthermore, why are you overly concerned about being loyal to "friends" who care little about your dreams?

Remember that you will need your energy as installment payments on your dreams. Dreams take work and perseverance. Do not waste another minute with dreamkillers. They are loose cannons in foreign territory, the Land of Dreams. Your first response to them should be a quick getaway. Your final response will be the attainment of your dreams.

Powerful Lessons Are Seen

What your children will learn from watching you fulfill your dreams means more than all the words you can speak and motivational pages that they can read. They will see the manifestation of dreaming big dreams, setting goals, and moving in the direction of fulfilling them.

Let your children see you keeping company with enablers. As they watch you interacting positively with others who have dreams, they will witness the embodiment of positive thinking. Little people have big ears. They enjoy listening to adults converse and they learn a great deal from tuning in on your adult discussions. Since they will overhear, let them overhear conversations of success. Let them overhear the exchange of positive ideas between people engaging in dream sharing and the promotion of one another's dreams. Let them hear "how-to" conversations. Let them overhear conversations about turning possibilities into realities. Let them hear what I call "communication reciprocity" (CR).

Strong friendships among positive young people are vital.

Communication reciprocity is sharing positive ideas with positive people, sharing dreams with other people who are dreamers and doers, and sharing encouragement that turns possibilities into realities. They listen and encourage you. You listen and encourage them. You share information with them and they share information with you.

As you practice CR with others, make sure that you are practicing CR with your own children. Be very careful not to sabotage their dreams. Sharing your hopes, dreams, and aspirations with your children will create a climate in your home that will encourage them to share their dreams with you. Don't be fooled. Children dream really big dreams. They dream big dreams because they have not yet known major failure and they still believe that anything is possible.

Children believe in magic and miracles and dreams. Too many adults, too many brothers and sisters, laugh at a child's dreams, as though they are too big, as though their dreams are impossible. Treat every dream that your child shares with you as a real possibility. After all, people do grow up to become researchers, scientists, physicians, nurses, astronauts, inventors, engineers, lawyers, social scientists, entrepreneurs, skilled tradesmen, film-makers, healers through medical research discoveries, governing officials, Supreme Court justices, writers, and the ones who taught them all—teachers.

Encourage your children to foster positive relationships with other young people who have visions of a bright future. Though it is true that you cannot pick your children's friends any more than your parents were able to pick yours, laying the groundwork for positive relationships in your daily life will add to your children's understanding of how to develop positive relationships in their lives. If you practice communication reciprocity, you will soon have the pleasure of watching your children do likewise. They will be able to discern enabling associates from disabling ones, and will be well on their way to fulfilling dreams.

These young people have a look that says they are ready to tackle anything that comes up.

CHAPTER SIX

Education Begins at Home

I send my child to school everyday and want him to do well. How can I make certain that he succeeds?

Wise and alert parents do not relinquish responsibility for their children's education. They recognize early on that it is a shared responsibility to see that their children receive a good education and develop a worthwhile value system. This is a joint challenge given to family, school, religious institutions, and community.

A child's level of educational success is determined by what he brings from home to the school experience and how the school experience impacts him personally.

Millions of children of all races enter formal schooling with very few experiences that would guarantee success. Such programs as Head Start are an effort to enrich the child's background and put him on a more equal footing with his peers who have had a wider range of learning experiences. Head Start today, like many other programs to help the disadvantaged, is in danger of being drastically reduced or cut out all together. This would be a serious mistake.

Your Presence Felt at School

Ideally, the home–school connection should be an unbroken circle that operates in the best interest of each child. But what should be and what actually is are two different things. To have knowledge of what is happening in your child's school, you must visit the school. Not only go to open house and Parent-Teacher Association meetings, but make it your business to visit your

A system of education is not one thing, nor does it have a single definite object, nor is it a mere matter of schools. Education is that whole system of human training within and without the schoolhouse walls, which molds and develops men. — *W.E.B. DuBois*

child's classroom sometime during the year.

When you meet your child's teacher and visit the classroom, the teacher is keenly aware that you are concerned about your child's academic achievement and overall development.

Parents who never come to a meeting or visit their child's classroom are perceived as being uninterested. Children of uninterested parents sometimes receive a little less attention than children whose parents take the time to get involved.

No clear-thinking parent should ever turn his child over to a school system and remain detached from the activities that occur in the school environment. Parents need to be involved and know what is included in the curriculum. Every parent should make sure that her child has a dedicated, competent, and culturally aware teacher.

Continuing Presence at Home

Coming home from school each day marks not the end of but a continuation of what transpired in the classroom. That four-letter word, t-i-m-e, is extremely important. Time must be spent with the child in the evening. It is not so much the length of time as the quality of time spent. Anyone who is successful will tell you that their wise use of time is part of their success story.

Establishing a *Home Study/Sharing* (HSS) time at the beginning of the school year is essential. It is a powerful way to help your child get off to a good start as you follow up on activities, assignments and concepts introduced in school.

Children function best in an environment that is orderly and predictable. It is essential to have a definite time and place for home study/sharing. The benefits derived from this allocated time will be proportional to both your and your child's commitment to HSS time or the lack thereof.

The television and radio should not be on during this time of serious home study and sharing. Television should enhance our experiences and add to our enjoyment, not dominate family life. Too often television inhibits interaction and conversation between family members. Children who view television for long periods of time tend to become dull and unresponsive. They have become so programmed to the television that they often have trouble concentrating on real-life situations.

Take charge. Who paid for the television, radio, and music equipment in your house? Children may balk when you first establish a home study/sharing time, but they will soon adjust, enjoy, and look forward to this time designated for mind expansion and family togetherness. Not only will their academic performance improve, but so will their feelings of comfort and security within the family. If you are willing to work hard enough to

The television in the background is doing its part — it is off!

establish HSS time in your home, it will go a long way toward combating negative outside influences.

No matter how tired you are after working all day or night, you still need to spend quality time with your children. Remember that they have also been to work. Their job is to go to school and learn. They need you to assist them in the evenings when necessary, and to keep a watchful eye or lend an encouraging word as they study and complete assignments.

This special time will help you determine what is going on at school and also gauge your child's rate of learning. Too many parents wait until a report card full of unpleasant surprises comes home. Then they angrily rush to school wanting to know what is going on. Rushing to school after the fact and in a fit of anger, cussing and threatening the teacher, does not help your child. Granted, there are times when teachers have been known to spring unpleasant and sometimes unfair surprises on students. But by and large, this will happen less if parents are willing to stay involved in their child's education on a daily and weekly basis throughout the entire year.

Your child's progress will be determined by his understanding of the importance of an education and by his commitment to study and learn. You can help foster his success by being an involved parent. The earlier you start, the easier it will be and the greater the rewards.

CHAPTER SEVEN

African American Families

Historical and Cultural Meanings of Family

A child is influenced positively or negatively by everyone in the home and community to a greater or lesser degree:

Parents • Peers • School • Teachers • Religious Institutions • Relatives • Caregivers • Adult Role Models • Neighborhood Institutions • Neighbors • Strangers • Government Policies.

Some cultures understand and give weight to nontraditional family structures. Many African cultures recognize that a family goes beyond the limited, and often less effective, perimeters of what most western cultures perceive as a family. In fact, African Americans built families out of their African traditions and developed new family patterns that were structured out of necessity during our enslavement in America.

As mothers, fathers, and children were torn apart without warning, they were forced to make other "family" arrangements. In order to preserve sanity during this period of unbearable suffering, these courageous human beings formed workable family units for survival and comfort. When a father was sold down the river or stolen under the cover of darkness, another "father" appeared at the cabin door to offer solace, comfort, and love. When a motherless child showed up at the plantation with an odd assortment of other "chattel property," some field hand, whose back wore an entangled maze of ribbons, reached out to that orphan child and took him into his cabin.

These families did not easily articulate the characteristics of what we commonly think of as a healthy family structure. Their limited and broken vocabularies did not know the words safety, nurture, and stability. But their hearts knew all too well the meaning of such words as violence, disease, hunger, toil, and loneliness. In spite of all these hardships, they managed to put together families. These creative structures offered what they could of safety, respect, trust, and fleeting moments of happiness. Many of the family patterns that were established during our enslavement several generations ago still exist today in modified variations.

Until recently, African-American children were taught to respect close family friends in the same way that they were taught to respect blood kin. Young children often had trouble distinguishing who was really an aunt, uncle or cousin. Children addressed these extended family members as Aunt Josie, Uncle King, or Cousin Liz. This inability to differentiate who was blood and who was not made little difference. Often children were practically grown before they realized that a family member was not related by blood, but rather was part of a wider circle of loving adults who were determined to keep them on the straight and narrow path. And instead of diminishing the respect and love that the children felt for the extended family member, this revelation only served to reinforce positive attitudes and feelings that they held for these "aunts" and "uncles" who helped them reach adulthood safely.

The blurred lines only enlarged the circle of love. Children sometimes viewed this big circle as a disadvantage when they were scolded by an "aunt" or "uncle" or were followed home by an extended family member who issued a negative report. This bad news usually resulted in a punishment or an old-fashioned "whupping" that would either make you mend your ways or be more cautious in the future.

The necessity and wisdom of such structures conveyed a knowledge and understanding that one or two people could not raise children as well or as effectively as a wide family circle that protected and steered children successfully through uncharted waters. Not only did children enjoy a high level of comfort in this circle, but they received support and guidance from many adults who had their best interests at heart. Children learned to respect and accept many people. They also developed coping skills by observing and then emulating members of the extended family.

These structures, born out of suffering, served as bastions of strength and aided black survival over the centuries. Elderly people served as matriarchs and patriarchs of the family and held a special place of honor because they had "weathered the storm." Children were taught that age should bring honor and wisdom; they often witnessed wisdom spill from the lips of family elders. Even young children soon recognized that this wisdom did not come from books, but from living.

Today's African American Family

As massive efforts are undertaken to reexamine today's African American family and to bring stability to the center of family life, definitions vary as to what constitutes a strong, healthy family.

Most people can tell you what they think a family ought to be, coupled with ideas of what roles various family members should assume. And though these ideas and opinions vary, certain characteristics should dominate most family structures.

The family should provide a safe and nurturing environment. It should offer stability and consistency in day-to-day living. The family should be able to function successfully without the constant threat of turmoil or violence. Adults in the family should be able to deal with and work through crisis situations as they arise. A high level of love and trust should permeate the family and give its members a sense of well-being.

Ideally, when the family offers a nurturing environment and a safe haven from the outside world, children move through the various stages of growth and development without major incident or trauma. Unfortunately, societal conditions today allow fewer

Extended family groups can offer children the benefit of many adult role models to learn from.

and fewer children to get through the developmental years without some major incident or crisis.

One of the best ways to increase the chances of success and lessen the dangers of failure is to broaden family circles.

This cannot always be accomplished. But when it can, having other extended family members and close friends to help nurture and guide our children increases success in raising them and lightens the load of child rearing, though the parents still carry the major load and responsibility. Those who refuse help and guidance from grandparents and other loving associates are either extremely brave or foolhardy.

The need for extended families becomes more apparent as young upwardly mobile families settle in many different areas of the country due to job transfers and promotions. If you are one of these families that has located far away from blood relatives, you could certainly use the love, support and guidance of an extended family in cities distant from your roots. Adopting some "aunts," "uncles," "cousins," and "grandparents" for your children should prove especially beneficial.

Extending your family allows your children to be positively influenced by good role models and to learn more of life's lessons. Remember, you can't teach them everything.

Traditional and Non-traditional Families

Today, as in slavery time, not all families consist of the traditional structure that is often visualized when the word family is mentioned. Therefore, it is important to recognize that many non-traditional family structures can be very effective in raising children.

Most children tend to view their own family structure as quite normal since it is the one that they have known. But when adults raise an eyebrow, question a child's family structure, or look down on a child from a non-traditional family structure, then problems may arise.

Today's non-traditional family may include children being raised by a grandmother, an aunt and uncle, a family friend, or foster parents. The blended family is very common as a divorced parent marries another divorced parent and both bring their children at least part of the time to a common household. Two single parents decide to tie the knot; a single parent marries a widower, and so on.

Many people who have grown up in non-traditional family environments exhibit great self-confidence, a high level of trust, and strong feelings of self-worth that enable them to succeed. It isn't so much the structure of the family, but the stability and love found within the family that makes the difference.

The concept of extending the family is wise and practical today as it was many years ago. Only recently have social scientists and mental health professionals begun to extol the virtues and benefits of the extended family. They have come to recognize what the African/African American family knew centuries ago: Children need a wide circle of love.

✤

A word of caution: Allowing others to assist in your child's development does not mean blind trust. Remember that some people have bad motives for befriending you and your children. Study people carefully and observe their habits, not their words. No matter how slick, people usually betray their ill-intent in one way or another. Do not ignore warning signs. Be a keen observer in order to ward off problems before a crisis situation develops.

Proceed cautiously and slowly. Remember, you have much to lose if you are too trusting. Everyone is not an honorable person no matter what their profession; and no profession is exempt. Child abusers have been found among the ranks of teachers, ministers, priests, community leaders, and babysitters.

Family Variations

Fewer families today consist of mother, father, and children. Children can grow up healthy, happy, and sane in family structures other than what many people recognize as the traditional family.

Consider the following family structures that might be found — and not just among African Americans — anywhere in America today:

- mother/father/children;
- mother/children;
- father/children;
- mother/grandparent/children;
- father/grandparent/children;
- guardian/children;
- aunt/children;
- uncle/children;
- aunt/uncle/children;
- mother/father/children/other relatives;

- relatives/children;
- stepfather/mother/children;
- stepmother/father/children;
- older sibling/younger siblings;
- family friends/children.

No matter what their structures may look like, loving families that affirm children enjoy a higher level of success in rearing children.

The Building Blocks of Child Development

The poem "Building Blocks," on the following page, symbolizes the essence of our children's lives; for the lives of children are much like the building blocks that they use in play.

Children start out fresh and new, viewing the world in awe and wonder. All that adults need do is capitalize on their infantile enthusiasm by properly guiding and nurturing them. The natural curiosity of children and the innocence of an unblemished view of the world are the easiest traits upon which to build as we seek ways to ensure their road to happiness, success and fulfillment.

Parents and caregivers must handle carefully the fragile building blocks that are our children's lives. In this way, each child will be able to partake of the rich bounty that helps make America great.

When the blocks are strong, secure and built upon a firm foundation, our children will use them, at the appointed time, to take the helm of leadership in an unbroken circle.

BUILDING BLOCKS
By Kristy R. Holley

Once upon a time, when you were a little one
the world seemed fresh and vivid
to your newborn eyes

and your tiny hands reached out
to those around you,
searching for the provider
of guidance and inspiration

and as time passed,
you learned to take small steps
then bigger ones
and you laughed and cried, and
explored your surroundings with enthusiasm

We gave you color blocks
that you could build and learn,
forming unique arrangements
that sometimes only you
        completely understood.

And now, my child
the time has come that you must take even bigger steps
as you explore
        new and different surroundings

Your blocks, too, have changed
as you must use
blocks of courage and honesty
and
blocks of pride and determination
to build and learn
until you discover the unique arrangements
      of your happiness

and it is then that you must remember the world
as first seen through newborn eyes
and you must reach out once again
to those around you —
only this time as the provider —
of guidance and inspiration

The world awaits . . .

(Kristy R. Holley is a native of Montgomery, Alabama. She received her B.A. in English from Spelman College, Atlanta, Georgia. She is currently a third-year law student at the University of Georgia, Athens. She fills much of her spare time writing poetry and participating in African dance. Kristy also enjoys reading fiction and poetry.)

SECTION II

Education

CHAPTER EIGHT

Historical Perspectives

Education — A Ticket to Success

When the newly freed slaves ventured off the ruined planta-tions of the South to make their own way, they were not only minus the promised forty acres and a mule, but they were also illiterate and unlearned. What they lacked in formal learning, they had to make up in common sense, raw intellect, intuition, and keen observation.

Looking toward the future, they knew that their survival and that of future generations would depend upon their ability to work the land successfully. Tilling the soil was certainly not foreign to them. It was the main thing that they had been allowed to do. Another factor for success was less familiar to them, yet they recognized its importance. They knew that learning to read and write was a ticket to a brighter tomorrow. This desire to gain knowledge from books was very strong within our ancestors. For the most part, books had been kept out of slaves' hands very successfully. In some Southern states, a slave caught with a book could face severe punishments or even death. Punishments were also meted out to anyone caught teaching a slave to read and write. (It is interesting that the same tactics were used against blacks in South Africa during apartheid.)

Given this legacy toward their efforts to read and write, these unlearned men and women understood the importance of learn-ing and moved quickly after emancipation to establish shanty schools for their children. Their valiant efforts did not go unno-ticed by those who knew the power of words. Enemies of African-American education worked to keep books out of the hands of former slaves and their offspring. Schools were burned and teachers, both black and white, were run out of communities or worse. Though often pathetic looking little structures, these early schools were usually crowded with eager pupils ranging in age from young children to adults. However, the school year was often short due to the demands of the planting and harvesting seasons, when students had to join their sharecropping parents in the fields. Many a bright young man and woman had no chance to fulfill their genius. We can only imagine what they might have become given the chance.

Despite violence, poverty, and constant interruptions during the school year, efforts to educate these newly freed slaves and their sons and daughters prevailed. Teachers, poorly paid at best, sometimes ended up as volunteers because there was no money at all to pay them. Yet they continued to teach under dire conditions. These early educators understood that the best hope for African Americans lay in the education of their children.

Not only did visionary individuals establish one-room schoolhouses for basic learning, but some went a step further to establish the forerunners of today's black colleges and universities. Often supported by northern philanthropists who provided the land, buildings, initial leadership, and teachers, African American schools sprang up throughout the South. These early institutions, initially established to take students a few steps higher than the basic fundamentals taught in the one-room schoolhouse, served as training grounds for doctors, lawyers, teachers, preachers, agricultural experts, and skilled craftsmen.

> You can't make nothing without a good education.
> — *Osceola McCarty*

Over the years, these schools, founded on the fringes of slavery and sustained by sheer determination and perseverance, grew into colleges and universities. Far removed from their meager beginnings, they offered broad and comprehensive programs of study. Their record of success in educating and graduating the largest

Although the end of segregation opened the doors of all colleges and universities to African Americans, the historically black campuses still offer advantages and an environment which is preferred by many students.

number of African American students is unsurpassed. And though the black college campuses of today cannot compete with the average predominantly white campus in terms of physical facilities, their efforts remain unabated in their struggle to attract and prepare students for the workplace and for further studies. [See resources.]

Black colleges often lack adequate dormitory space to accommodate the growing number of students seeking admission. These colleges also must compete with richly endowed colleges for outstanding professors to teach students. Many professors found on African American campuses are there for reasons other than professional benefits, financial gain and prestige. Many are there because they see their tenure on historically black campuses as a way of giving back to the African American community. Their greatest satisfaction comes from watching many students enter as timid freshmen, but leave as self-assured, confident, and learned young men and women ready for the challenges that await their generation.

A Mandate for Learning

If the penniless, unlearned, and newly freed slaves could envision and establish schools for their children, surely we as their descendants can recognize and embrace the importance of education for our daughters and sons in today's highly competitive, complex, and technological world. We enjoy advantages and opportunities that our ancestors could not have imagined.

Preparing our children for the future means making sure that they obtain a strong fundamental elementary and secondary education. But obtaining this formal education is really phase two. Phase one is the education that precedes and runs parallel with the formal school education. Phase one takes place in the home. This means that parents have the major responsibility for seeing that their children receive a good education.

If one considers the state of public education today and the intentional and unintentional roadblocks that are built into educational systems, no clearthinking parent can afford to leave the education and development of their children totally in the hands of formal educators and educational institutions. To do so is to court disappointment and disaster.

Public school systems are under scrutiny and attack across America for failing to adequately educate students. All of the blame for failing to educate children cannot be placed on the schools. Schools have increasingly become dumping grounds for the myriad problems found in society. Schools should not be asked to, nor are they capable of rectifying the failures of society as a whole. Educational institutions lack the resources and know-how to solve social problems.

In truth, the degree of success of any school system is tied to the amount of parental and community support it receives.

On the other hand, students who fail in school have seldom voluntarily chosen this path. Instead, they are pushed out by poverty, neglect, and institutional walls and barriers that impede their progress and make it increasingly difficult for them to find their way through the educational maze. Much of what passes in schools for education is anything but education. It is sad to say, but many schools are holding tanks that encourage lock-step thinking. Schools can and must be turned into centers of learning for all children. With the help of parents, they can become centers for creative thinking. This can happen if parents are willing to activate phase one of their children's education. Once phase one is activated in the home, it must be followed by considerable and ongoing parental involvement in phase two which takes place in the schools.

> Do not let yourself be overwhelmed! If you are wise, strong enough to survive the threatening atmosphere of the streets, then channel that same energy into thriving in that same atmosphere at your school. — *Bill Cosby*

Few African Americans are born with silver spoons in their mouths. Few inherit well-established businesses. Thus, we must pursue education as a way to become successful. If we are to participate fully in the life of this nation, we must continue to make education a top priority. Let's face it, in the twenty-first century, no one with an eighth-grade education is going to be put in a position of power and responsibility. They may not even find a job.

We must also recognize the need for us as adults to continue our education. We must not limit our learning to the information put before us in public and private educational institutions. Real education comes when we can and do seek information, knowledge, and truth independently of a classroom. Education must be ongoing and lifelong. As we continue to learn, we are better able to impress upon our sons and daughters the importance of getting the best education that is available to them.

The extent of your involvement in your child's education will, to a large degree, determine her school success and her future success beyond the formal school experience. We must understand that what happens in the schoolhouse does not end at the school door each day, but will have profound and far-reaching effects throughout life.

Your responsibility as the first teacher can prove rewarding and enjoyable if you understand and assume the challenge of partnership in your child's formal education. Don't waste time looking for some mystical plan for educational success that will fall upon your child's head like manna from heaven. Magic tricks and wizardry will not create educational success. Recognize that your child's quality of education and level of achievement will be determined by his will to succeed and your commitment and involvement in his education.

[See activities for educational involvement, page 118.]

Historically Connecting Past and Present

No other Americans' history prior to coming to these shores is more interesting and intriguing than that of African Americans. And no other ethnic group has experienced the level of degrada-

Give children a fair chance, and they will learn.

tion, violence or lack of promise that accompanied our forced entry onto American soil.

All of this history, before America and since America, must be taught to our children. We must come to terms with our history, as must the entire nation, no matter how wretched and painful the history is. We must teach our children — and white children must be helped to understand this — that the shame was in slavery, not in being a slave.

If we start early enough, our children will understand the meaning of time and where they fit on the historical timeline. Not only will they understand that they are a part of an ongoing saga, but they will know that they can write future chapters of success for our people. They will realize that starting behind always means having to work a little harder and run a little faster in order to catch up, to remain even, and then to move forward collectively.

Our children must be taught that they are descendants of a people that survived some of the worst atrocities in recorded history. Our very presence today is a testimony to strength, endurance, and resilience. This is their legacy.

Too many African Americans see our beginning as our entry to America as slaves. Nothing is further from the truth. Our history is ancient and awe-inspiring. African Americans must rethink our beginnings by reading from a growing body of literature about the history of our people. When armed with this body of knowledge, we can properly instruct our children about their history and heritage.

Helping children understand the history of their people is one of the best ways to build self-esteem. When children have pride and self-esteem, they can be motivated to meet new challenges. Children who understand that they stand on the shoulders of strong ancestors who survived subhuman conditions will not resort to violence, crime-filled lives, and low-achieving lifestyles.

How Do I Locate Information About African American History?
While much of the history of black people has been lost,

stolen, distorted, and "borrowed," there is a growing body of literature and historical information available to those who wish to be enlightened. Start with the library. There should be a substantial collection of books and novels by and about African and African American history. If you do not find a substantial collection of books in your library, ask the librarians to order some. Think of the stacks of books as your tax dollars lined up on the shelves. If you do not see any of the books you are looking for, then your tax dollars are being misappropriated.

Most major cities now have at least one African American bookstore; many also accept mail orders. Most general bookstores feature an African American section. They will also order books not found on the bookstore shelves.

Much historical information is available today because of the pioneering research of such scholars as Carter G. Woodson, W.E.B. DuBois, John Hope Franklin, John Henrik Clark, Horace Mann Bond, E. Franklin Frazier, Ben Johannan, Ivan Van Sertima, Maulana Karenga, and Asa Hilliard. Through their research and the research of many other scholars, this body of knowledge continues to increase. It is readily available to individuals, schools, library systems and organizations interested in learning about the history of Africans and African Americans.

Why Can't I Just Depend On The Schools To Teach African/ African American History To My Children?

Many attempts to include African/African American history in the school curriculum have been feeble and half-hearted at best. Until recently, textbooks and school curricula excluded the history and contributions of African Americans. There was an occasional footnote listing some contribution by an African American, but for the most part the contributions of blacks have been excluded or underrepresented.

It is also sad but true that many of the early references in textbooks about blacks were derogatory and outright lies. When mentioned at all, blacks were portrayed as docile, slow, stupid, shiftless, and lazy. Especially in Southern school systems, textbooks portrayed slavery as benign and depicted slaves as happy and care-free and as being well provided for by kindly masters. Generations of schoolchildren, black and white, absorbed these flagrant lies. To add insult to injury, these untruths were reinforced in the homes of many students, both black and white. Many whites were made comfortable believing these distorted versions of history, and many blacks had been sufficiently brainwashed and beaten down to accept untruths. Sadly, much of the bigotry and prejudicial attitudes still infecting many whites can be traced to the distorted information written in textbooks as truths.

In the past few decades, the African American scholars named above and others, and many white scholars such as C. Vann Woodward, George Tindall, and others, have corrected much of the historical record of slavery and segregation. Important new research continues to emerge in the areas of African American families, community organization, worship, political activities, and economics. But, especially among older people, many of the old myths and half-truths continue to shape thought and action. There is much work still to be done.

Educators who understand the importance of history find ways to incorporate African American history into the curriculum throughout the school year, teaching in a manner that is inclusive of all Americans. Unfortunately, too many feel no such commitment. They either do not understand or refuse to acknowledge the ramifications of excluding a large segment of the population.

What About Black History Month?

When Carter G. Woodson envisioned a weeklong celebration during the month of February to commemorate the achievements and contributions of African Americans, few blacks dared entertain the idea of completing high school, not to mention college, which was a remote and abstract concept for all but a lucky few.

Separate facilities were the law of the land, few African Americans were allowed to vote, and night riders were still running rampant through the South. Yet Negro History Week took root in 1926 and has been a month-long celebration since 1976.

At times, I have thought that if the contributions of African Americans had been written accurately into the story of America, there would be little need for a Black History Month. But after reflection, I realized that inclusiveness has not been the case in the past and often is not the prevailing attitude today. The misdirected attack on multicultural education is a perfect example of continued attempts to exclude or downplay contributions of African Americans and other ethnic groups that helped build and shape our nation. In fact, the story of America cannot be adequately and accurately told without telling the complete and unaltered history of African Americans and their inextricable connection to the development of this nation.

> Sing a song full of the faith that the dark past has taught us. Sing a song full of the hope that the present has brought us. — *James Weldon Johnson*

We must teach children that this month-long celebration is vital for many reasons. It is first and foremost a celebration of our survival. Millions died prematurely because of slavery, either from violence, disease, or deprivation. So we are the children of those who were strong enough to survive.

Black History Month is a celebration of our patriotic service in every war this country has fought from the War for Independence to Vietnam and today's conflicts around the globe. It is a celebration of our efforts to survive during and after the war between the North and South, a war fought not for our freedom, but for preservation of a union that was divided by ideology and economic systems.

This is a celebration about holding to hope in times of despair as roaming night riders brought murder and mayhem under the cover of darkness. They put fear in the hearts of black men and women well into this century so that the victims would remember to stay in their places.

But some of those brave black souls had amnesia about staying in their places. Frederick Douglass forgot. Likewise, W.E.B. DuBois, Marcus Garvey, and Ida B. Wells Barnett forgot. And because they forgot, Vernon Johns, Rosa Parks, Martin Luther King, Jr., and Fannie Lou Hamer forgot. By forgetting, they opened up a new era for this country that pricked the conscience of the nation and led to laws to end discriminatory practices and brutal mistreatment of African Americans.

This is a celebration of contributions in medicine, science, music, visual and performing arts and literature. Our long list of achievements and contributions has benefited all Americans.

Black History Month is a celebration for our children so that they can develop positive self-concepts as they recognize African American achievements. Children who know their history will build upon it. Understanding their past will help them choose books over guns, delay parenthood until an appropriate time, and embrace healthful lifestyles over unhealthy ones. They will reject drug addiction and, instead, pursue learning that leads to achievement over failure.

It's a celebration of our continuing triumphs in the face of those who would clump every African American under one label instead of recognizing the uniqueness of each individual, no matter the race. It's a celebration that we must remember our ancestors who sacrificed, made do with what they had, and worked jobs that others were unwilling to do, so that their children and grandchildren would enjoy the fulfillment of dreams.

Today, those children graduate from more than a hundred predominantly black institutions such as Hampton, Morehouse, Spelman, Tuskegee, Clark-Atlanta and Kentucky State. They also attend formerly all-white institutions such as Stanford, Harvard, Brown, and Yale as scholars, not just as athletes.

So yes, February is a month to pause, reflect, and celebrate our contributions. It is a time to study and learn, along with our children, more about a history that gives us much cause to celebrate as we look toward the promise of a brighter tomorrow.

CHAPTER NINE

Multicultural Education

Multicultural education is a recent movement to incorporate into school curricula information about the contributions of all racial and ethnic groups. A multicultural approach embraces respect for people of all cultural, ethnic, racial or religious backgrounds. It promotes the right of all cultures to exist in harmony.

The multicultural movement resulted from African American protests about distorted portrayals and/or the exclusion of blacks and ethnic groups from textbooks and history lessons. Now, school systems across the United States have developed or are working on comprehensive multicultural curricula that will accurately reflect the diverse population of the United States.

This movement was long overdue. The old curricula focused on whites of European origins to the detriment of almost everyone else. Yet it is vital for their feelings of self-worth that all children see themselves mirrored in the curriculum. We must recognize that self-esteem and academic achievement are clearly and closely linked.

Not only should the curriculum be inclusive, but the teaching and administrative staffs should reflect the diversity of the students. We can go a step further and say that all children are deprived in a school setting that has a non-diverse teaching staff and administration. When only whites stand at the front of the classroom and in administrative positions, it sends a loud, clear and faulty message that only one group is capable of running the show. Such a hierarchy may cause African American children and children of other ethnic groups to internalize feelings of inferiority while Caucasian children may develop false feelings of superiority. All ethnic groups should be included in the curriculum.

**Diversity in the classrooms leads to stronger education, which
leads to a stronger nation.**

The multicultural effort, though late in coming, is hailed by
thinking people who recognize that the American story is not the
story of one group. Over a period of time, curriculum inclusiveness will help reduce ignorance, stereotypes, and fear of other
groups different from one's own.

School systems and the teachers who implement the curriculum will give life to this multicultural mandate if they take the
challenge seriously. In time, multicultural curricula will be commonplace and a fundamental part of the teaching learning process.

How Can I Make Certain That My Children Learn Their History?

No matter what efforts schools make to expose children to a
multicultural curriculum, the primary responsibility still rests
with you, the parent. You are the responsible party that must see
that your children learn about their history and the myriad
contributions that we have made worldwide and in American
society.

As you and your children explore African/African American history, view your exploration as a wonderful challenge to learn more about our contributions. There are dozens of things that you can do to enrich and expand your cultural background.

Begin with a simple list of African American books. (See Resource Section for children's reading list). Many books are written for different age groups and reading levels in which African American characters are cast in a positive light. Read some of the books together to build your child's interest. You should also encourage independent reading. Let your son give you an oral report on what he has read. These reading sessions do not have to be lengthy, and the discussions that follow should prove interesting. In fact, reading and discussing what your son or daughter has read will lead to many interesting conversations apart from what is written in the book. Parent/child discussions are an excellent way to build good communication between you and your children.

African American points of interest continue to grow. Visit some of these historical sites every summer or during winter or spring breaks. [See Resources.]

Involve your children in culturally aware community-based programs, church youth groups, and rites of passage programs. These programs, established to help build self-esteem, pride and an understanding and appreciation of our rich heritage, also help prepare and educate African American children for the future.

Though the number of after-school and weekend programs continues to grow, the need is greater than the availability of such programs. If your community or church has not established meaningful programs for children and adolescents, why not team up with other parents and organize a group to meet their needs?

What Can I Do To Help Encourage Multicultural Education In My Child's School?
1. Check the curriculum to see if it is multicultural.
2. Examine textbooks to see if all racial and ethnic groups are included.

3. If the curriculum is not inclusive, make an appointment with the local school administrator (principal or headmaster) to discuss your concerns. Go alone or join with several other parents for a group conference. There is strength in numbers.

4. If you do not receive cooperation there, take your concerns, as a group, before your local board of education.

5. Organize a letter-writing campaign to the local newspaper or spearhead a telephone blitz by parents, churches, other organizations and concerned citizens to school board members.

6. Encourage faculty and staff training in cultural awareness and diversity in order to better understand and relate to all students. Once the school system has embraced the idea of a multicultural curriculum, it must be implemented at the local school level.

The following list includes activities that you can suggest to your child's teacher to insure infusion of a multicultural curriculum:

- Classroom and schoolwide multicultural bulletin boards
- Supplemental reading material, if adopted texts are deficient in multicultural representations
- Assignments that include oral and written reports about various racial and ethnic groups
- Multicultural sheroes/heroes biography reports that can be compiled into classroom anthologies.
- Select multicultural supplemental storybooks and novels
- Design multicultural comic strips
- Multicultural murals
- Student design of individual posters of their families
- Read and memorize poetry of many ethnic groups
- Plan a multicultural food fest. Students bring food from their cultural backgrounds
- Select or write plays with African American, Hispanic, Native American or Asian American themes
- Study various family structures

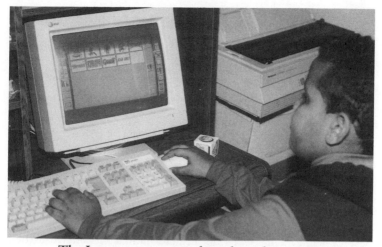

The Internet can expand modern classrooms.

- Gather oral histories from elderly in family or community
- Hold multicultural student forums
- Listen to music of various ethnic groups
- Invite adults from different ethnic backgrounds to speak to class on any number of subjects, e.g. careers, culture, travels
- Produce videos that celebrate diversity
- Use the Internet to communicate and share information with other teachers, students and schools in different sections of the country.

❖

Schools today can no longer ask students to leave their cultural roots and diversity at home. Forward-looking school systems recognize that they cannot miseducate and turn out students that are one-dimensional clones of what one group perceives as American.

We are all Americans and we must all learn to accept our differences as positive forces upon which to build inclusive communities that will lead to a stronger nation.

CHAPTER TEN

Keys to Educational Success

Personal Commitment to Your Child's Education

Ask any parent what kind of education they want for their child and they will tell you without hesitation that they want the best available. They want an education that will increase their child's chances of success in life. Yet, too many people fail to realize that a child can never receive the best education possible unless they as parents are actively involved in their child's education. Parents must understand that securing the best education for their child involves not only school days spent with effective educators, but exposure and experiences that occur before and after the school day. Effective education must come from many areas and encompass the sum total of our experiences.

Parents who are sincere about education must have a high level of commitment to spending quality time with their children. The time spent must go far beyond viewing television together or saying a few words while involved in other distracting activities. Time must be spent interacting with the children. The parent must be willing to see that their children are exposed to the world beyond the local neighborhood.

> I leave you a thirst for education. Knowledge is the prime need of the hour. — *Mary McLeod Bethune*

If you are committed to your child's education, you must be willing to give of your time in the home and community by helping create a learning environment independent of what happens at school. Parents from other ethnic groups make certain that their children have excellent educational opportunities inside and outside the classroom, and we must do the same. We must make sure that our children can take advantage of all available opportunities so that they will be able to compete.

The Power of Words

Have you ever sat mesmerized by a public speaker? Have you ever been spellbound by a person who could speak poetically and weave words into pictures? This ability to captivate an audience is the art of effective and powerful communication. Even if the speaker has some natural ability — the "gift of gab" — you can be certain that this level of articulation is no accident. Their ability to express thoughts and ideas clearly and succinctly has been mastered through practice. They almost always have the right word to convey a particular thought or idea.

Speakers who hold you in their spell are usually somewhat animated, though not necessarily so. They speak clearly so that you can understand every word. Their phrasing paints visual images. Without even realizing it, you may shut out distractions around you because you are so heavily focused on the speaker. As you listen to articulate speakers, you probably draw conclusions about them based on their ability to work words like putty. Your impressions about them may or may not be accurate. But rightly or wrongly, people are judged by their ability or inability to speak well. Though the art of eloquent speech may be only one of many signs of intelligence, it definitely carries considerable weight in our society. If you have the ability to speak well, you are automatically viewed as bright, smart, and going places. On the other hand, the person who struggles to articulate his thoughts may be just as intelligent as the master of words but will be judged by his inability to use language.

Unfortunately, people make similar judgment calls on children. Unfair though it may be, children are judged by their ability to express ideas. Many educators believe, and some studies substantiate, that language use is an early indicator of school success.

Rewards come to the confident child who communicates well.

Developing an Articulate Child

I believe my child is intelligent and would like him to have good use of the language at an early age. What should I do?

Since a child first learns language from his parents, how you respond to your child and the dialogue between the two of you will determine his initial language development. Therefore, if you want your child to communicate effectively, you must talk, talk, talk with him. This will give him a sizeable vocabulary at a young age. Furthermore, talking with your child will increase his understanding of the world around him. It will enable him to grasp concepts that are fundamental to reading success when he enters the formal school setting. Let's skip the "babytalk" with three- and four-year-old children. Limited babytalk can be used with very young children, but parents should also talk to them using regular language and voice.

It is easy to recognize children who have been involved in dialogue. It is just as easy to spot those who have been ignored or simply parked in front of a television. There are great benefits to be gained from selective television viewing, but nothing takes the place of human interaction. Children who are involved in conversing respond easily, enjoy a greater vocabulary, tune into their environment, and portray greater confidence. By contrast, children who have been shunted aside may appear withdrawn or show aggressive behavior, give one-word answers when talked to, and seldom portray a high level of confidence. Some parents have done such a poor job of communicating with their child that the child comes to school not knowing his given name. They will only answer to nicknames such as Spike, Skip, Sweetthang, Honey, and Pookie. Please! A child entering school should know her name. A nickname is all right and it is acceptable for other students and the teacher to call the child by her nick-

> O God, give me words to make my dream-children live. — *Joseph Seamon Cotter, Jr.*

name, but it is unacceptable for a child to enter school not knowing her real name.

Enunciating (speaking clearly) is important. The ability to express thoughts means little if no one can understand what you are saying. Children learn to enunciate by listening to their parents and peers. Do not hesitate in correcting speech patterns. When children mispronounce words, tell them how to pronounce the word correctly and praise them for the corrected pronounciation. Correct your child as often as necessary.

> Strive to make something of yourself; then strive to make the most of yourself.
> — *Alexander Crummell*

This will help him understand that you expect his best at all times. With practice, good speech patterns can become a habit just as bad ones so easily do.

Whatzup With Slang!

My preteen/teenager is using slang all the time!

And so did you at that age. How soon we forget. Using slang is perfectly normal. Using slang is part of the world of teenagers. It defines their space. They use it as leverage in a world where they are not quite adult, but often are asked to act as though they are. The use of slang separates "them" from "us."

It is quite normal and the "in" thing to speak the language of their generation; it would be a little unusual if your teenager did not.

There is no need to be overly concerned about your teen's use of slang. If she already has a good basic foundation for standard language expression, she will be able to move back and forth between the language of her peers and the more standard language of adults.

Regional Accents

People from my part of the United States speak with an accent.

Yes, I'm sure they do. Everyone speaks with an accent.

Regional accents add interest to the spoken word. Can you imagine anything duller than everyone speaking with the very same accent, be it northern, southern, midwestern, or eastern? To ridicule someone who has a different regional accent than your own is to expose a very narrow view and a lack of appreciation for the diversity of language and people.

A fun game to play with your child is to listen to people with different accents and later try to determine what region of the United States they are from.

A Place for Black English

What about Black English?

Spice! Black English adds spice to the language. Just as regional accents add interest to spoken language, so do the unique expressions and vernacular of African Americans add spice to American Standard English. Black English and many of its unique expressions permeate the American language.

Our African oral language traditions have enabled most black Americans to take language, modify it, shape it, twist, curl and turn it into unique expressions and give fine or delicate shades of meaning to hundreds of words and phrases. This ability to knead the language like dough adds excitement to standard spoken English. In fact, I just can't imagine a day without a good Black English expression.

The most fascinating aspect of the use of Black English is the ability of millions of African Americans to move between Black English and Standard English. Many of us have grown up using heavy to moderate black vernacular, yet can shift in a split second to Standard English patterns. This is another example of black survival skills.

> Dialect or the speech of the people is capable of expressing whatever the people are. — *Sterling Brown*

More than likely, you and your children use speech patterns flavored with Black English. Keep your spice, but make sure your children know and understand Standard English. They do not

Children can be "as smart as a whip" in ways that don't show up easily on standardized tests.

need an unnecessary handicap by being limited to Black English. Help them understand that using standard language effectively is a powerful tool by which one can advance economically and socially. The ability to use Standard English may well prove to be his most valuable asset. His inability to use Standard English may prove to be his worst liability.

Many Kinds of Smarts

The Intelligence Factor. In his book, *Frames of Mind,* noted research psychologist Howard Gardner has developed and advanced a theory of multiple intelligences. He has divided our intelligences into seven areas.

Gardner has expanded the usual way of looking at intelligence, which is linguistic intelligence (verbal and language) and logical/mathematical intelligence (numbers and logic). To these areas he has added spatial intelligence (ways of seeing images and pictures), musical intelligence (ability to perceive and produce melodies and rhythms), bodily-kinesthetic intelligence (ability to perform well physically), interpersonal intelligence (ability to understand and work with people), and intrapersonal intelligence (ability to be in touch with the inner self).

Many people have always known there are different types of "smarts" or intelligence. Gardner has validated that knowledge of multiple intelligences in a credible manner through research.

How many times have you heard someone describe a man or woman in the following terms: "He can play just about any instrument he picks up." "She's got a voice that belongs at the Met." "You can't help but like him because he's so kind to everybody and makes you feel special." "What a physique, and he's so athletic." "She is so calm and seems to be at peace with herself and the world." "She seldom gets ruffled." "There isn't anything that he cannot make with his hands. He can build things, repair anything in the house, and on top of that he's quite an artist. Have you seen his latest painting?"

All of these expressions are describing the multiple ways people demonstrate intelligence.

Unfortunately, schools tend to evaluate students on the first two types of intelligence, linguistic and logical/mathematical, which are more easily measured. While some school systems are beginning to recognize the other types of intelligence, by and large schools are designed to teach linguistic and logical/mathematical intelligences and this will not change in the foreseeable future. There-fore, while recognizing that human beings have multiple types of intelligence, we must continue to help children do their best in the areas that are used today to measure their intellectual development.

> Nobody's ordinary. Each one of us is special and it's the coming together of alla that that makes the world so fine.
> — *Ntozake Shange*

CHAPTER ELEVEN

Reading

The Importance of Reading

Today has been called the information age. As we move toward the twenty-first century, the explosion of information and knowledge continues at an incredible rate. And though we can now get much of our news from television and radio, and though we can keep in touch with family, friends, and business associates by telephone, voicemail, answering machine, and even videophone, we still need to be able to read well and read *critically*. The ability to read critically is such an important skill. A person who can't read critically will go through life at the mercy of demagogues, con men, and other manipulators of various persuasions.

To foster good reading skills and enable critical judgment in our children, we cannot start too early. And there is no more valuable gift that we can give our little ones. Parents enjoy lavishing their children with gifts for birthdays, holidays and other special events. Yet long after material gifts are worn out, discarded and forgotten, children who have been given the love of reading will still have that ability and it will grow with them through a lifetime, feeding the mind and freeing the spirit.

Establishing a daily shared reading time will prove enjoyable for both of you. Beginning the reading experience early, long before the children enter school, will give them a head start toward educational success. It also makes them understand early that books and learning have an important place in your household.

When you begin reading to babies and toddlers before they can recognize letters and words, they will soon make the link between the words you are saying and the symbols on the page.

Have you ever noticed young toddlers "pretend" reading? They are demonstrating their understanding of the connection between the spoken and written word. Their "pretend" reading is showing you that a foundation is being laid for real reading that will soon follow.

Reading time should be fun for you and your infant or toddler. Babies enjoy being read to and will become excited, kicking and babbling, when you share picture books with them.

Reading time need not be lengthy. Just ten or fifteen minutes is usually adequate for smaller children. As children mature and become more and more interested in exploring the printed page, the length of time spent reading will increase and gradually they will begin reading to themselves.

The importance of reading cannot be overemphasized. Read to your child or listen to him read every day. Reading time is an excellent way to bond with your child. As importantly, it is a good time to instill and reinforce values.

The Importance of the Library

Libraries are vital community resources that are often underused and undervalued. Yet these are some of the most important public institutions found in local communities. Many citizens, African Americans among them, seldom or never use this wonderful community resource.

Only in the past three decades have many communities opened their "public" libraries to African Americans. Before segregation barriers fell during the civil rights movement, when communities did provide a library for blacks, it was most often small and poorly stocked. Now, African Americans have access to libraries across the nation. We must use these facilities and teach our children to use them if we are to be learned men and women, as well as competitive in a tight job market.

Besides reading to children at home, we must take the time to carry them to the library. Whatever the subject, from astronomy to zoology, it can be found in the library system. Remember that a portion of your paycheck is deducted for taxes that are used to support your local public libraries. Why not reap the benefits of your tax dollars? Select library books, records, tapes, and games that your children will enjoy. If you have not visited a public library lately, you will be pleasantly surprised by the services and information available.

Positive African-American Images in Reading

The number of books by and about African Americans has grown rapidly in recent years. This groundswell of African American literature for both adults and children was sorely needed.

As noted earlier, for too long there was a vacuum of positive black images in our educational system. Practically every school in America was devoid of curriculum materials that positively depicted African Americans in everyday life situations. Not only were basic reading books totally Eurocentric, but all of the materials and textbooks throughout the curriculum omitted visual images and pertinent information regarding contributions of people of color.

> My challenge to the young people is to pick up where this generation has left off, to create a world where every man, woman, and child is not limited, except by their own capabilities.
> — Colin Powell

This same paucity of positive black images also existed in adult and children's literature. It is amazing that black children over the years have achieved as well as they have, rarely seeing themselves mirrored in textbooks and literature. Though they achieved, how much more pleasant the journey of learning and how much higher the level of achievement might have been if black children had seen themselves mirrored in readily available reading material.

Today, more and more new and well-established African American authors are finding avenues to showcase their talents and expose the world to the rich and varied stories of their people.

When a child's imagination is pricked by a good book, he will spend less time involved in passive activities and more time interacting with good reading material. Though television serves an important place in American life today, it should not be the center of our existence. Television itself exhibits too few positive

Worlds of opportunity await the reading child.

images of African Americans. Every ethnic group has a criminal element, but a greater and more significant number of achievers; and they are the people that should be highlighted by the media. You can find these achievers profiled in books that you can use to entertain, educate, and motivate your children. You just might inspire yourself, too.

Read to your children. Read to them in order to open doors of opportunity that might otherwise remain shut. Reading helps children understand the world as a big and exciting place. The ability to read well often determines the degree of school success. Books contain a special magic. When children explore the pages of books, what they find often leads to interest in many subjects. Young minds can have their imaginations fueled with possibilities of what they can become and of vast career choices. Becoming an avid reader can help children set and attain high goals now and in the future. [See Resources.]

Ten-Point Plan to Cultivate a Love of Reading in Your Children

1. Select a book suited to the interest and age of the child.
2. Sit close to the child or let him sit in your lap.
3. If the child wishes, let her hold the book.
4. Read with expression and enthusiasm. Your reading voice should sound very much like your regular speaking voice.
5. Point to the words that you are reading. (Later the child should be taught to use a book marker, placing it under each line and moving it down as he completes the line. This aids fluency in reading and keeps him from losing his place.)
6. Stop frequently and talk about the pictures.
7. Be relaxed. Avoid rushing through the book.
8. Help the child relate to events in the story in a personal way.
9. After you have finished reading, discuss the story/book.
10. Children usually have a favorite book. Be willing to reread it many times.

CHAPTER TWELVE

Fostering Educational Success

Attitudes toward School, Learning, and Peers

Educational success is much more than academic achievement. The whole child must be involved in order to have a successful educational experience. This experience must involve mind, body, and spirit.

One of the most significant factors determining how children will do in the educational arena is the attitude that they bring with them. Everyone has an attitude. The question is "What kind of attitude does your child have toward school, learning, and his classmates?" Your son's attitude will determine whether he moves toward success or failure.

Many a bright child underachieves simply because she entered school believing that she could do as she pleased. Children should be taught at an early age that everyone has someone to answer to, and ultimately that someone is the self. People have the highest level of happiness, satisfaction and achievement when they understand that the greatest responsibility is to self. If you want to achieve, you can. If you believe you can, you will. Children must be taught that there is a time for work, study, and play. Everyone is best served when each human being respects the rights and opinions of others. They need to understand that agreement is not always necessary, but that there is usually a way to disagree agreeably. It is rather obvious that a large number of adults and children in today's society know little about negotiation or the art of working out differences (conflict resolution). For many, the way to solve a dispute is simply to beat or kill the person that got in their space or made them angry.

Strong male role models are especially important for showing children that nonconfrontation does not equal weakness.

Many gun-toting adults and young teens never learned that problems can be resolved peaceably. Children can be taught from a very young age, beginning with the "terrible twos," how to resolve conflicts nonviolently.

Many parents have taken what they think is the easy way out by failing to address negative attitudes in their children. As a result, thousands of children are bringing more than school books to school each day. Many are bringing nasty little attitudes which they direct toward their peers and teachers. Bringing a bad attitude to school will hold your child back. Discuss frustrations with him so that he can learn how to work through his problems in ways that are not confrontational or threatening to others. We must teach our sons and daughters that there are solutions to most problems. They also must learn that no one is always right and that they cannot always have their way.

Getting physical with or killing another human being is a

tragic outcome for people who have never learned to resolve problems in a peaceful manner. We must teach children that violence in society starts and stops with individual behavior. They also need to understand that those who commit violent acts today are the ones most likely to be in the headlines tomorrow as another victim in this escalation of violence that has gripped the nation.

We must teach our sons and daughters how to resolve conflicts peacefully.

Several steps can be taken to resolve a problem:

1. Identify the problem or conflict
2. Take control of our anger and avoid seeking revenge
3. Hear what the other person involved has to say
4. Be willing to compromise
5. Discuss ways to resolve the problem so it does not reoccur

Discuss troubling situations with your child and help him come up with acceptable solutions. Children can be taught to work through their problems in an acceptable manner. Negative attitudes in very young children can often be traced directly to the home. If your child's attitude is negative, it's a good idea to check your own.

Teach your children that instead of packing knives and guns to school, they need to be armed to the teeth with self-respect, a will to succeed, and a positive attitude. Success stories are written with positive attitudes. A positive attitude will enhance and increase your child's chances of acquiring the education that will enable him to be a winner. Being a winner and becoming successful is the best revenge.

Empowerment through Education

If we as a people are to control our own destiny, enjoy a high quality of life, and be a positive force to be reckoned with, we must pursue education as our avenue to self-empowerment.

Our children must be mentally prepared to meet the challenges put before them. There is no skirting the fact that education still offers most African Americans our best way to improve our condition in American society.

We must teach our children to honor and respect their families. They must be willing to stand alone and not succumb to peer pressure. They must learn to be determined and not give up quickly. They must recognize that the road to success is not without trial and error, and even tribulation.

> Not to know is bad; not to wish to know is worse.
> — *Wolof proverb*

We must study with them the lives of great women and men who have contributed to society on a grand scale. Careful study will reveal that most of these achievers endured hardships and great sacrifices to reach their goals. They often were misunderstood and ridiculed for taking the positions that they took because being great or setting lofty goals means going it alone much of the time.

Whatever career paths our children choose will require an education. Whether they pursue higher education, apprentice for the trades, or choose a military career, they will need a strong fundamental education.

We must prepare them to become leaders of the highest caliber, leaders who are not only learned in various fields, but who will not abuse power and who will bring integrity to and be worthy of the positions of responsibility that they will hold.

As we guide our children in their educational pursuits, we must continue to expand our own base of knowledge. We must not limit our learning to the information put before us in public and private educational institutions. Recognize that we are truly educated when we can and do seek information, knowledge, and truth independent of an instructor.

Education must be ongoing and lifelong. Here some ideas for fostering educational success and family togetherness:

1. Be committed
2. Give of your time
3. Explore African American culture

4. Learn about other ethnic groups
5. Visit historic places
6. Work to improve communication skills
7. Have command of standard English
8. Read to your child to foster love of reading
9. Engage in dialogue with your children
10. Be selective in television viewing
11. Tell children stories of your childhood
12. Take children to museums, concerts, plays
13. Teach children games that you played as a child
14. Have family pantomimes
15. Go hiking, biking, fishing
16. Visit nature reserves
17. Encourage collecting (rocks, stamps, dolls, action figures)
18. Invest in a set of encyclopedias
19. Use libraries
20. Explore positive African American images in reading and the media.
21. Work on interpersonal and social skills
22. Buy a computer
23. Read and memorize poetry
24. Subscribe to your local newspaper.
25. Purchase newspapers from other cities at a local bookstore
26. Encourage diary or journal writing
27. Play educational games
28. Visit your child's class
29. Review his work daily
30. Praise often

SECTION III

Community

CHAPTER THIRTEEN

Building Community

A community can be defined as a place where a number of people live and have common ties. They share the same local government and should be bound by the same laws. They often share similar interests due to their environment.

But the above definition does not encompass all the nuances that individuals think about when they consider the meaning of a community. How would you define the ideal community that you would want for yourself and your offspring?

Let's go several steps beyond a dictionary definition. A good community shares common goals for the collective good and is able to pull together to achieve those goals. It is inclusive of all the dwellers and lets them have a real part in building the collective community but it also allows individuals the freedom to shape their personal lives and those of their families. Such a community is a place where people can work, play, and grow spiritually and intellectually. Such a community provides a sound fundamental education for its young people and also offers continued learning opportunities for adult citizens.

> For my people lending their strength to the years, the gone years and the now years and the maybe years. — *Margaret Walker*

Within that community, common experiences encompass happiness, sadness, joy, sorrow, and prosperity. The life of the community is sustained by the birth and development of the young so they can grow into adults capable of assuming their own responsibilities within the community.

Most people in a good community are intent on building and

sustaining institutions that promote a high quality of life. They also recognize the importance of focusing on the children as a way of perpetuating and improving their communities.

We are individually and collectively responsible for the kind of community that we live in by what we do or what we fail to do. We are also individually and collectively responsible for the kind of community that our children will inherit.

All those aspects of community are probably universal. If you could talk with people in Mexico or Portugal or Senegal or Sweden about their communities, you would probably find very similar attitudes and goals. The need for community transcends place and race.

In the United States, African American communities have historically faced some unique challenges. First slavery and then segregation severely restricted our forebears in their efforts to build strong communities. Knowing the obstacles they faced should give us even more respect for what the previous generations of African Americans were able to accomplish.

However, understanding history will not change it. What must we do today to build strong African American communities that will impact the future and determine the opportunities for our children and grandchildren?

We must be determined and relentless in our efforts to reclaim and restructure African American communities. The problems that we face cannot rest on the shoulders of a few community leaders or government programs. We must develop shared goals to invigorate and clean up communities that are beset by crime and devoid of economic development.

Talking will not reclaim or build strong communities. We already know what the problems are. Developing a plan of action is the challenge. Talking about what should have been, what could have been, what used to be, and what might have been will not move us toward reclamation. We must come to terms with our plight and move beyond the petty chasms that divide us and wait to engulf our children and their hopes and dreams. We must embrace actions that will lead African American children to light, happiness, and to the fulfillment of their potential.

What can you as an individual do? You can start by making a list of all the organizations and institutions in your community. Why do they exist? What are their goals? Are they building community or just sustaining themselves for selfish purposes? Are the organizations committed at the grassroots level to building community or are they centers for self-aggrandizement?

Are you a part of any organizations that have very narrowly defined goals and purposes? What have they done for the community lately? Do they have programs to support and encourage African American children? Do they support African American enterprises? Why do they exist?

If any of these organizations do not have, as part of their mission, the building of a better community for all people, and especially for children, they probably would not be missed if they disappeared today. If you are a part of such an organization that lacks focus or has a self-serving agenda, you would do well to withdraw membership and use your awareness and talents with organizations that are doing real work.

Building community begins with dedicated individuals and strong family units that are headed by parents who assume responsibility for their children. Add an extended family, a vision for the future, and organizations and institutions with a sense of purpose, and the result will be good communities in which to raise our children.

Moving toward Peace and away from Violence

Violence is everywhere. It is in the home, the streets, our schools, and even in our houses of worship. It permeates our lives even when we try to ignore its presence. If we lock ourselves inside our homes and turn on the television, it is there. If we pick up a newspaper or magazine, it is there. If it has not visited our immediate family, most of us know someone who has been a victim.

African Americans may be affected by violence more than any other group. Many of our communities are economically depressed, drug-ridden and crime-infested. Sometimes we can only shake our heads and wonder how American society became so base and violent.

While we are in search of some solutions, let's look at a few facts:

- Violence is not new to America. She was founded violently. Early settlers took the land by force from the indigenous people. They were uncompromising, ruthlessly aggressive, and unwilling to share the land and resources with those who were already here.
- From the birth of this nation, her policies have often been hawkish. Whatever she wanted, she took. And whatever rules she set, others countries were "encouraged" to comply or risk the threat of violence.
- People of African descent were transported to these shores in a violent manner and kept in bondage by a violent system.
- Television and movies glorify violence. Hollywood producers, actors, and actresses live opulent lifestyles paid for by giving society heavy doses of on-screen violence.
- Of course, we are the ones that have allowed our children unrestricted viewing of violent movies to the point that many of them have been desensitized to suffering, pain and death.
- The media offer graphic portrayals of violent crime scenes and give more details than is necessary to tell a story.

Add to all of this the reality that millions of African Americans suffer from low self-esteem, self-hatred, alienation, and hopelessness, and we have a dangerous combination. Young people who should have the greatest amount of hope are often the most hopeless. Because of their feelings of worthlessness and despair, they have little regard for human life.

The aberrant behavior that has been adopted by large numbers of African American males is a result of historical amnesia. Children who understand the history of African Americans in this country will not kill another human being for a pair of athletic shoes, rob senior citizens, or fill their veins with chemical poisons. Nor would they risk life, limb, and imprisonment to make quick dope dollars. If they understood their history, they would take the high road to success. But they have no sense of their history because no one has bothered to teach it to them. Parents and community institutions have failed them.

> The ultimate weakness of violence is that it is a descending spiral, begetting the very thing it means to destroy. Instead of diminishing evil, it multiplies it. — *Martin Luther King, Jr.*

An example of historical amnesia running full circle is today's violent crime in the streets of Little Rock, Arkansas. It is not fair to single out Little Rock from hundreds of other communities whose problems with street crime are just as bad or worse, but there is a special heartrending irony in Little Rock. There, in the fifties, National Guardsmen had to be called out to protect the African American children who integrated Central High School. Today in Little Rock, the problems are more from internal forces within the black community than from the external forces of the fifties and sixties.

It is important not to give up, but to develop aggressive plans of action in African American communities all across America. When heads of households, educational institutions, religious and civic organizations begin to develop aggressive plans of action that teach children about the African American experience, then children will not suffer from historical amnesia. Having an increased understanding of their legacy will enable them to move away from violence and toward peace.

Reclaiming Our Communities

In spite of a growing number of African Americans who are working tirelessly to reclaim black communities, many cities remain hubs of violence, crime, and decay. A growing number of African Americans who have made it economically are heeding the call to return to African American neighborhoods and help rebuild them. They are devoting a great deal of energy and countless hours working with African American children who desperately need role models. They recognize that the severity of the problems that grip African American neighborhoods has turned many of them into not only physical but psychological war zones.

Along with individual efforts, plans and strategies to stabilize our neighborhoods are being devised by civic groups, social clubs, Greek letter organizations, and other organizations such as YMCAs located in black neighborhoods.

The black church has become a major player in this concerted effort to reclaim our neighborhoods. Following a lull after the Civil Rights Movement of the fifties and sixties, the black church is beginning to reassert itself and wield some of its considerable power. That power can help stabilize and regain control of black communities.

Many churches which had limited their function to serving as Sunday morning emotional release centers are now developing meaningful outreach programs. They offer support groups for recovering drug addicts, feeding and clothing programs for the poor and homeless, and adult literacy classes. Many offer health awareness programs that are so desperately needed in African American communities.

Churches and other organizations have also instituted Rites of Passage programs. These programs bring teens together with positive adult role models who can help smooth the transition from childhood to adulthood. Rites of Passage programs emphasize that along with racial pride goes racial responsibility.

Recognizing the importance of education, a growing number of churches and community centers offer after-school tutoring programs. Tutoring programs serve as support centers for the academic challenges that children face on a daily basis. Too many African American parents do not take advantage of tutoring opportunities for their children. They seem not to understand the advantages and impact of tutoring. With adequate attention in a one-on-one or small group tutorial environment, children can quickly move to higher achievement levels.

The work of churches and other organizations is being undergirded by other groups such as neighborhood associations. These associations do not exist just to clean up litter and paint over graffiti on public walls. They have joined ranks with local law enforcement officers to eliminate vice and crime in their neighborhoods. They have been known to shut down dope dealers and run them out of their neighborhoods. Unfortunately, this cesspool of crime just moves around and usually sets up shop in someone else's neighborhood. This means that problems are not solved, just passed around. It also means that residents in all neighborhoods must be vigilant in looking out for the crime element that is looking for a home.

Add the enthusiasm of high school and college students who participate in mentoring programs and cross-age tutoring programs, and you recognize that there is a movement sweeping the nation; a movement bent on reclaiming black communities and making them prosperous and safe places to live and work.

In spite of the combined efforts of various groups and organizations, the success of our efforts to save our children and reverse the decline of our neighborhoods will be determined by the condition of individual African American families. Heads of households must accept a new level of responsibility. They must take charge of the family and do whatever is necessary to secure the future for our children. They must carefully chart a course that will allow their children to grow up healthy and sound in mind, body and spirit.

A Massive Effort

In October 1995, one million African American men assembled in the nation's capitol for a day of atonement and reconciliation. These men arrived in Washington, D.C., with a sense of purpose because the call was clear and relevant as we face a multiplicity of problems in African American communities across this nation.

Their presence carried broad and personal implications for African American people. Those who gathered sensed the need for greater personal commitment and increased responsibility for the African American family. The broader implication spoke to their willingness and determination to impact their local communities and neighborhoods.

Thousands of African American men who attended the Million Man March are now serving as catalysts to other African American males who have vacillated over whether to get involved in their respective communities, share ownership of local neighborhoods, and assume greater responsibility for their families. They also may cause some African American males to lay down their personal arsenals and cleanse their veins and brains of chemical poisons, while others, for the first time, are grasping the need for economic empowerment.

Change will not come overnight, but change is coming. African American communities will be reclaimed and rebuilt by those who share a vision and a willingness to do whatever it takes to save them.

CHAPTER FOURTEEN

Strengthening Our Communitites

Ridding Ourselves of the Crab Syndrome

Individual members of any group of people that has experienced enslavement and the degree of violence and oppression that African Americans have must work extra hard to develop a positive mindset. Part of the residual effect of our slave history is to feel diminished as persons. Anyone who feels unworthy and less deserving than people of other races will certainly not feel that he can achieve the good life. He will also feel that others in his race are undeserving of good.

This feeling of unworthiness manifests itself among African Americans today in a crabs-in-a-barrel mentality. How does it work? If one crab crawls on top of the pack to try to get out, the other crabs simply pull him back down. The crabs crawl over and over atop one another but nobody gets out.

Though the crab mentality may be less a problem today than in the past, it is still around. It has remained in effect by the negative statements made in front of and to our children. Just as other aspects of our culture are passed down to the next generation, so is the crab mentality passed from generation to generation. Even people who claim to be aware of the crab mentality unwittingly practice it, while others knowingly embrace this racially defeating attitude.

Eradicating the crab mentality means putting an end to envy and jealousy toward other African Americans who are as successful or more successful than you. Eradicating the crab mentality means redirecting negative mental energy, attitudes, and actions into positive actions that will lead to self-fulfillment.

Most of us know people who waste precious time discussing how someone acquired their job, home, car and other material possessions. They badmouth someone else's promotion or raise instead of using their own energy to be involved in self-help or self-improvement activities.

Why be jealous of someone who expends tremendous effort and untold hours to make a success of running a business? Our entrepreneurs need our financial and moral support, not envious gossip about their backgrounds. Young people who struggle to climb corporate ladders are under tremendous pressure to succeed. They need our encouragement, not our petty envy.

Jealousy and envy would not exist if more people recognized what goes into being successful. There are few overnight success stories; it just appears that way to outsiders. People who are successful almost always have made tremendous sacrifices, worked hard, and made wise choices about their lives and careers.

African Americans who suffer from the crab syndrome would do well to realize that whatever successes some other African Americans make, those successes tend to be small in comparison to the overall U.S. economic statistics. Why would African Americans want to deny their own a few slices of bread from such a huge loaf?

> I leave you the challenge of developing confidence in one another . . . [You] must develop more confidence in each other in business. This kind of confidence will aid the economic rise of the race by bringing together the pennies and dollars of our people and ploughing them into useful channels. — *Mary McLeod Bethune*

The only way that we can break this negative cycle is to point out successful individuals to our children. We must tell them that success comes about by hard work, sacrifice, and tenacity. Now and then a little luck enters in, but luck can't be depended on. We must also teach them that the success of each individual becomes a part of the overall success of African American people, and the success of our people adds to the overall strength of the nation.

If we recognize and respect successful African Americans, our children will develop appreciation for hard work and dedication, along with a determination to succeed.

Economics Need Not Be a Foreign Word

The economic power of African Americans is a virtually untapped resource for community development. We are fifty million or more strong and share an estimated combined income of approximately $400 billion. Imagine the awesome potential of such an economic base if properly exploited.

We must find ways to keep black dollars in the black community longer instead of seeing them make an immediate exit.

We must take four basic steps toward economic empowerment. First, we must know and patronize African American-owned businesses for as many basic services as possible. If unavailable in the African American community, then we should use the services outside of our communities. Imagine what would happen all across America, if eighty percent of African Americans sought the services of black-owned businesses for just one week.

Second, more African Americans need to pool resources and start competitive businesses in many areas. Mom and Pop stores served a useful purpose in their day, but they can hardly compete with today's supermarkets and megastores. We need different business models in our communities. We have the knowhow and intellect for developing competitive businesses. What we lack is an understanding of what such businesses could mean to the collective African American community.

Third, we must emphasize black economics to our children. They must see us purchasing goods and services from African American establishments, even if it means driving across town. They must also see our ongoing efforts to establish businesses. And, we must discuss with our children the importance of and potential within the African American community for using our income to generate prosperity and wealth for our people.

Fourth, the thousands of young, gifted African Americans who graduate from colleges and universities with baccalaureate, masters and Ph.D. degrees must be made to feel that they can build financial dynasties with our backing. All of their brilliance that is being tapped by mainstream corporate America could also be used to build an economic force to be reckoned with. It can be built only if we encourage them to explore independent business opportunities, and then support their efforts with some of the billions of dollars that we let slip through our fingers and out of our communities.

The point of doing business in the African American community is not to penalize non-African American business owners. But, notwithstanding the combined economic clout that we possess — those billions of dollars mentioned above — it remains a reality that a huge economic gap exists between African Americans and their fellow citizens. As a group, African Americans are below the national average in per capita income, home ownership, overall rate of employment, levels of supervisory and management positions, business ownership, and on and on.

Walk into any mainstream corporate headquarters, large banking institution, front office of a major retailer, insurance company, law firm, or whatever, and you will see few African American faces. Certainly the picture looks better than it did in 1950 or 1960, but we are still a long way from equal employment opportunity. The exceptions are found in black-owned businesses, black-directed banks, offices of black professionals, and government offices in those places where African American populations are high enough to guarantee equal participation in the electoral process.

Therefore, it stands to reason that if we want to open up more management and supervisory positions to African Americans, then we should open up more black-owned and black-run businesses. This will not only provide jobs for our deserving young people, but it will provide them with experience and know-how that they can take to mainstream corporate positions, and it will lead to the creation of wealth. In America, wealth equals power and influence, so as we develop a stronger African American economic base, we will find that we can participate in discussions that are now closed to us.

Finally, although it is important to recognize our young people who have earned academic distinction in business or professional courses of study, it is equally important to recognize and support those who have learned trades and crafts. African American people fill a multitude of positions in the workforce from entrepreneur to blue collar worker, from manager to professional, who are steady in their work and honest in their lifestyles. Skilled plumbers, mechanics, nurses, technicians, clothing and shoe makers, and others, not only master difficult vocations but are often small business owners/managers as well. They provide good lives for themselves and their families, and they play a vital role in the overall African American economy.

✛

In order to move toward economic empowerment, there are several questions that every African American should consider:

1. What percentage of my income is spent patronizing African American establishments?
2. Do I try to find out if services that I need are available from an African American business?
3. If I find that the services and products that I need are available from African American businesses, do I patronize them?
4. What do I tell my children about African American businesses?
5. If I do not patronize any African American businesses, why not?
6. If I patronize African American businesses, how can I encourage other African Americans, as well as people of other ethnic groups, to do the same?

It makes little sense to rave and complain about other ethnic groups setting up shop in African American neighborhoods if we are unwilling to take the most fundamental steps to empower our own economic development.

The best is yet to come for African Americans as we establish black enterprises and demonstrate our confidence in ourselves by collectively supporting them.

Who Are the Role Models for Our Children?

"I see you and I follow you." That is what young children will do. They will take their lead from you in a way that older children will not. As children grow older, they are more easily influenced by their peers and by what they see on television and in movies. This means that parents must set examples and instill values while their children are at an impressionable age.

Besides looking to their parents as examples, children also look at other adults that they admire and respect. Recently there has been considerable discussion concerning the lack of good role models for African American children. Is there really a lack of good role models, as some contend, or are we looking for role models in all the wrong places? We often point out historical figures from which young people can draw strength and pride, yet their lives carry a certain abstraction for children. Children need present-day role models with whom they can have real contact.

> I am not a role model . . . I am paid to wreak havoc on a basketball court. Parents should be role models. Just because I dunk a basketball doesn't mean I should raise your kids.
> — *Charles Barkley*

Many of us look to our famous contemporaries as role models for our children. But celebrity alone is not a good criterion for choosing role models for African American children. We might be better off pointing out local citizens whom we know something about and with whom our children might realistically identify than celebri-

Young black men can be very effective role models.

ties who have achieved fame yet sometimes lead bizarre and immoral lifestyles, and who do little or nothing for the African American community. We need to hold in high esteem those individuals who act as glue in our local communities. Look around at the everyday citizens who are quietly going about the business of building stable communities.

Let's not dishonor past generations who lacked opportunity for an education by looking down on or snubbing people who are hardworking or earn a living by the sweat of their brow. While it is all right to admire and respect people who seem to be successful, make sure that your admiration and respect are based on such traits as their humanity toward others, integrity and their efforts to move all people forward.

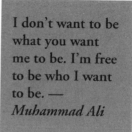

I don't want to be what you want me to be. I'm free to be who I want to be. — *Muhammad Ali*

Be careful not to confuse intelligence with a degree. Many people who are lettered are no more intelligent, and often less intelligent, than someone who is not lettered. Yes, we need our sons and daughters pursuing higher education, but along with that pursuit, let's encourage the cultivation of the best qualities that can be found in human beings. Let's teach our children to be compassionate, generous, tolerant, patient. Let's encourage a high level of integrity and emphasize the importance of service to others.

American society in general and black people in particular are impressed with ostentatious symbols of wealth. Many of us are more impressed with flash than with substance. Jewelry, gold chains, furs, designer labels, fancy cars and big houses do not indicate human virtue. While there is nothing wrong with accumulating material possessions, they should not be our focus or reason for living. We must emphasize issues of substance that do not carry a price tag. No monetary value can be placed on virtue, education, service, perseverance, hard work and compassion for humankind.

As your children look around for role models, make sure that they can start with you. One of the highest tributes that a parent can receive is having a daughter or son state that you are their role model. What an honor! What a responsibility! What a challenge.

A Legacy To Build Upon

The following list contains the names of men and women who were enslaved, and the names of many of their descendants, their children, grandchildren and now great-grandchildren. These African Americans, from every cross section of life, have made significant contributions to our nation. When one inspired or courageous human being does something of note, the ripple effect is pronounced and all of us are positively affected by their actions.

Besides the physical characteristics of their people, they carry the genius, strength and hope of African people who endured, persevered, never gave up and rebounded time and time again.

> Not to know what one's race has done in former times is to continue always a child. — *Carter G. Woodson*

Our forebears carried the torch and handed it to their children of promise who took it and ran with it. They carried a torch that still burns brightly with creativity and both raw and refined talent. They perfected the dance, the song, the instrument. They have used the sword, the pen, brawn and brain, eloquent tongues for freedom and rich voices to make known the plight and condition of their people and to express the pain and joy in their souls.

Many risked life and limb and sacrificed both so that those of us who follow can claim God-given rights to life, liberty and the pursuit of happiness. In spite of the struggle and difficulties in reaching their goals, I doubt any would change their place in the annals of history.

African Americans have made wide-ranging contributions to American life. We have given our nation our best in many fields such as education, philosophy, law, medicine, business, science religion, the arts—both visual and performing, music, sports . . .

As we read about and study the lives of these great men and women with our daughters and sons, let us abhor and work to stop the degenerates and criminal elements among us who would destroy the hard work and make folly of those who paved the way for our advancement.

Not only must our children learn about their contributions, but they must recognize that the torch is now being passed to their generation to add to those contributions in their own unique way.

Explore their lives with your children. Draw strength and determination from their examples.

There are hundreds of other names that are not included. You and your children can add additional names to your own list.

African/African Americans Past And Present

Henry "Hank" Aaron
Na'im Akbar
Marian Anderson
Ella Baker
Ida B. Wells Barnett
Charles F. Bolden, Jr.
Sterling Brown
Ralph Bunch
Calvin O. Butts III
Elizabeth Catlett
Joseph Cinque (Sengbe Peih)
Eldridge Cleaver
Bill Cosby
Ossie Davis
Charles Richard Drew
Katherine Dunham
Duke Ellington
James Farmer
E. Franklin Frazier
Henry Gates
Frederick Gregory
"Mother Hale"
W. C. Handy
Dorothy Height
Zora Neale Hurston

Ralph D. Abernathy
Muhammad Ali
Maya Angelou
James Baldwin
Mary McLeod Bethune
Carol Moseley Braun
H. Rap Brown
Selma H. Burke
Ben Carson
Ray Charles
Septima Clark
Johnetta B. Cole
Benjamin O. Davis, Sr.
Ruby Dee
Paul Laurence Dunbar
Jean Baptiste DuSable
Medgar Evers
Ella Fitzgerald
Marcus Garvey
Althea Gibson
Bryant Gumbel
Alex Haley
Lorraine Hansberry
Matthew Henson
Jesse Jackson

Alvin Ailey
Richard Allen
Crispus Attucks
Benjamin Banneker
Guion Bluford
Gwendolyn Brooks
Ron Brown
Margaret G. Burroughs
George Washington Carver
Shirley Chisholm
John Henrik Clarke
Marva Collins
Benjamin O. Davis, Jr.
Frederick Douglass
W. E. B. DuBois
Marian Wright Edelman
Myrlie Evers
John Hope Franklin
A. G. Gaston
Sam Gilliam
Clara McBride Hale
Fannie Lou Hamer
Patricia Roberts Harris
Langston Hughes
Mahalia Jackson

John E. Jacob
Mae C. Jemison
John H. Johnson
Maulana Karenga
Martin Luther King, Jr.
Spike Lee
Claude McKay
Winnie Mandela
Benjamin E. Mays
Constance Baker Motley
Jessye Norman
Leroy Satchel Paige
Adam Clayton Powell
A. Phillip Randolph
Wilma Rudolph
El Shabazz (Malcolm X)
Mary Church Terrell
Harriet Tubman
Madame C.J. Walker
Maxine Waters
L. Douglas Wilder
Granville T. Woods
Andrew Young

Daniel "Chappie" James, Jr.
Jack Johnson
Barbara Jordan
Sharon Pratt Kelly
Lewis Latimer
Joe Louis
Ronald McNair
Thurgood Marshall
Arthur Mitchell
Elijah Muhammad
Hazel O'Leary
Gordon Parks
Colin Powell
Paul Robeson
Augusta Savage
Fred Shuttlesworth
Howard Thurman
Nat Turner
Margaret Walker
Cornel West
Daniel Hale Williams
Carter G. Woodson
Whitney Young, Jr.

Judith Jamison
James Weldon Johnson
Scott Joplin
Coretta Scott King
Jacob Lawrence
Elijah McCoy
Nelson Mandela
Jan E. Matzeliger
Toni Morrison
Isaac Murphy
Jesse Owens
Rosa Parks
Leontyne Price
Jackie Robinson
El Hajj Malik
Bessie Smith
Sojourner Truth
Alice Walker
Booker T. Washington
Phyllis Wheatley
Oprah Winfrey
Richard Wright

SECTION IV

Lifestyles

CHAPTER FIFTEEN

Lifestyle Challenges

Health statistics on the African American population are alarming, starting with an infant mortality rate that is too high and a life expectancy that is too short.

The African American population carries a risk for diseases and premature death that is disproportionately higher than any other racial or ethnic group in the United States. Cancer, diabetes, hypertension, kidney failure, heart disease, stroke, and AIDS shave years off the lives of many African Americans. By the time many of these conditions are diagnosed, disease has ravaged the body and the prognosis is bleak. Lack of proper ongoing medical attention often results in a late diagnosis of health problems that might have been averted or at least controlled had they been detected early on.

Aside from late diagnoses of health problems, lack of health insurance, and mistrust of medical professionals, many of our health problems can be directly traced to our lifestyles. We cannot control our genes, but we can control habits that wreak havoc on our health. We can control obesity, smoking, drinking, salt intake, sedentary lifestyles, fatty diets, hypertension (high blood pressure) and diabetes. Let's briefly examine a few of these lifestyle habits that have proven so detrimental to our well-being:

❖

SMOKING is bad for your heart and lungs. Furthermore, your smoke is bad for other people's hearts and lungs. Studies have proved that secondary smoke can be just as harmful to the non-smoker as to the smoker.

Babies and young children especially should not be exposed to secondary smoke since they are still growing.

More and more businesses are dealing with the problem of secondary smoke by banning smoking on the premises. The tobacco industry and hard-core smokers are waging a losing battle regarding smokers' rights. Eventually, all public smoking will be banned and if you still choose to damage your personal health with tobacco, you will have to do it in the privacy of your own home or outdoors.

To help a person kick the smoking habit, several pharmaceutical companies offer nicotine patches. This product gradually decreases the desire for nicotine. Patches are available through your physician. In some cases, they may be obtained through clinics at no cost for people who cannot afford to pay for treatment.

If you smoke, resolve to kick this deadly habit before it kicks you.

Most smoking parents say that they do not want their children to smoke. One of the best ways to discourage them from smoking is for you not to smoke.

❖

DRINKING ALCOHOL is the most widely used legal drug for people twenty-one years of age and older. If you must drink, know your limit. Recognize that though it is a legal drug, booze has caused more untimely deaths and wrecked more homes and marriages than all of the other illegal drugs combined. Understand the effect alcohol has on the body and mind, then make your decision as to whether you really need it and to what degree.

Like smoking, drinking is often a habit learned from watching

> Black people in this country . . . must stop drinking, we must stop smoking, we must stop committing fornication and adultery, we must stop gambling and cheating and using profanity, we must stop showing disrespect for our women, we must reform ourselves as parents so we can set the proper example for our children. — *Malcolm X*

older members of the family. It is still too often glamourized on television and in the movies. Do your children see you drink moderately, or do they watch you get "lit up?"

If you feel like putting one under the belt now and then, pick and choose when and where you will drink. Avoid the two deadly combinations—drinking and taking medication, and drinking and driving.

> Liquor talk mighty loud when it get loose from de jug. — *Anonymous*

Because the bottom line is profit, the alcohol and tobacco industries spend a disproportionate amount of money advertising in African American neighborhoods. They know that people who are on the bottom rung economically and living in poverty with high levels of unemployment will look for a quick way to drown their misery. Drinking heavily is one way to dull the senses and "forget" about the problems that do not have easy solutions.

In recent years, several African American groups have organized to fight the exploitation of their communities by the alcohol and tobacco industries. They have painted over billboard advertisements while calling for an end to excessive advertising of alcohol and tobacco products in African American communities.

✛

If excessive smoking and drinking don't get you, maybe your POOR DIET laden with fat and salt will. Let's face it, the average U.S. citizen has a diet too high in sodium (salt) and fat, but too low on fruits, vegetables and grains. African Americans are leading the pack when it comes to poor eating habits. We love lots of fried foods, tons of salt, red meat, pork, fast food, junk food, and, please, don't forget the hot sauce.

One of the saddest sights is to see uninformed or uncaring parents give their toddlers large bags of junk food to eat as a snack. These innocent toddlers walk around with bags half their size and munch out of them at will. This begins a long and unhealthy habit of munching on salt and fat-laden snacks that will manifest itself later in health problems related to poor diets.

In order to protect your children before they develop obesity and a host of other health problems often related to poor dietary habits, we must modify our eating habits. The change may come slowly, but measure it one day at a time. Many years ago, the relationship between certain diseases, diet and lifestyle was not firmly established. Today it is. If you will work to develop healthy habits and teach your child to do the same, you will see benefits early on and big dividends in later years.

A well-balanced diet will help your family maintain good health. Using the U.S. government's latest food triangle [*See* Resources], begin restructuring your family's diet today.

✛

A SEDENTARY (inactive) LIFESTYLE can be a timebomb. Just keep sitting and before very long your muscles will become soft and weak and your flab will become flabbier. Being a couch potato is no joke. It is a habit that will yield serious consequences in time.

All children and adults should be involved in some type of physical activity. Some form of exercise is a must to maintain a strong healthy body and mind. Much of the obesity found in children and adults can be traced to sedentary lifestyles coupled with poor diets, and topped off with lots of television viewing. Allowing your child to develop a sedentary lifestyle early in life will make it more difficult for him to maintain good health now and in the future.

> If I'd known I was going to live this long, I'd have taken better care of myself. — *Eubie Blake*

One exercise the entire family can participate in is walking or jogging. There is little expense involved other than a good pair of walking or running shoes. This is an excellent activity for the entire family and an opportunity to be away from the distractions of the television or telephone.

People who exercise lower their stress level and often cope

better when problems arise. Don't envy people who are sleek, trim and agile. Talk to them and find out how they do it. Then you "JUST DO IT" until it becomes a habit.

A Word about HIV and AIDS

The most recent alarming news from the Centers for Disease Control and Prevention in Atlanta states that AIDS is responsible for one out of three deaths among African American men between the ages of 25 and 44. AIDS caused 22 percent of deaths among African American women in the same age group.

We cannot think of this dreaded disease as a killer of homosexual white males. The HIV virus does not discriminate. Your chances of contacting this deadly virus increase with drug use and promiscuous sexual habits.

If this killer disease is to be brought under control, all citizens, including African Americans, will have to be educated about HIV and AIDS. Continued denial of how it is transmitted and who is susceptible will only lead to an increase in the mortality rate among young people.

"Just say NO to drugs and sex" slogans are not enough. Educating ourselves and our daughters and sons about this killer disease is one way to reverse the current statistics.

Issuing threats or just saying be careful is not enough. Abstinence from sex and drugs must be taught early. We must not downplay the dangers of risky behavior. We must speak of this killer openly if it is to be harnessed and expunged from society.

⬖

GOOD HEALTH should be high on our list in raising healthy African American children. Let's face it, we can push educational achievement and economic prosperity, but these successes are truly short-lived without the good health to enjoy our successes and prosperity.

We Are Sexual Beings

We are designed to be sexual beings by God. That will not change. However, our attitudes toward our sexual natures determine what we will do with this powerful God-given part of our being. Many parents feel comfortable talking to their children about most any subject other than sex. Yet it is a subject that cannot and should not be avoided. Parents can try to skirt sexual issues but eventually the reality that we are sexual beings forces the issue into the open. A lack of information about the human reproductive system and how it works can prove disastrous to young boys and girls.

Children sense early their sexuality. They do not think of it as good or bad; it just is. Yet it doesn't take long for children to form very definite attitudes about sex based on what image society paints for them. They quickly learn all sorts of names for genitalia and get the message that this area of the body is a taboo subject. Given the fact that they are going to learn some things about the sexual nature of human beings, doesn't it make a lot more sense for you to give them correct and proper guidance? If you bury your head in the sand, then "the street" will seize your opportunity to instruct them. How much better for you to give them proper instruction about this powerful and God-given part of our being.

If children are given a real understanding of sexual matters through parental instruction and guidance, they will come to the exact opposite conclusion of what "the street" will teach them.

Children should be taught there is a time in life for the fulfillment of sexual desires. Being sexually active as early as eleven is not in their best interest. Sexual activity will prove limiting, emotionally depressing, and dangerous when embarked upon too early. Having a baby at thirteen is not the happy event that it may prove to be years later when young people have matured and have had a chance to fulfill some of their early goals.

Helping children set goals early in life will encourage them to wait longer before they become sexually involved. Children who anticipate a bright future and are involved in reaching high goals that they have set for themselves do not want their dreams canceled or put on hold while they deal with the problems that come with immature sexual involvement and early parenthood.

What is your attitude toward sexual involvement of adolescents? Some parents are guilty of a double standard concerning sexual matters. Parents can no longer, nor should they ever have, send the message to their sons that it is just being "male" to go out and "get some," while telling their daughters to hold out as long as possible. All parents that are guilty of this skewed thinking must answer the following questions: If you encourage or condone your son's right to go out and "get some," from whom do you think he will "get some?" Whose daughter is to be the "some" that you think it is all right for your son to bang?

Remember that you will either address sexual issues with your children or they will receive all of their instruction from "the street," and the message it sends will not be the one that you want them to have. If you are truly at a loss as to how to approach the subject, seek help. There are good books on the market that will guide you. Use the books as a starting point, but above all stay within your value system on these matters. Couple what you read with common sense. Talk to your clergyperson regarding your concerns. Many churches are beginning to conduct workshops on sexual matters for adults, as well as children. If there are none in your area that offer instruction, make a suggestion that your church start an instruction group. Don't forget to talk to close friends about their approaches. Often we can borrow ideas from friends, then incorporate these ideas into methods that work for us.

Remember that the approaches you choose to educate your daughters and sons about human sexuality and the reproductive system are up to you. You should make the final decision on how such matters are presented to your child.

CHAPTER SIXTEEN

Give Children a Spiritual Anchor

Anyone who has lived a couple of decades knows that life can get rough. And rough times call for survival skills to get us through. People have many different ways of trying to make it through difficult times. In order to survive life's rough times and relieve stress, some adopt a physical fitness and/or sports regimen. Zooming around the tennis court returning balls to an opponent who has a mean backhand helps relieve stress. Dreaming of the hole-in-one or just working to improve your golf game is a stress reliever, while others may use racquetball for physical fitness and a natural high. Swimming, walking, jogging, playing a musical instrument, or listening to jazz, blues or classical music may also calm your frayed nerves.

Some of us talk out our problems or frustrations with a licensed therapist, while others use a friend as an inexpensive psychologist. Those of us who love to read may escape into the world of a good novel, while others seek inner peace and calm through meditation.

Whatever you do to survive the stresses of life demonstrates an effort to stay afloat and to cope with the curve balls life sends your way.

Though people embrace various avenues to escape stress and the pressures of life, there is a strong chance that you seek comfort and guidance through your religious beliefs and spiritual connections. Belief in a higher being and the practice of religion is a predominant way that many African Americans sustain themselves in trying times. In fact, we have sustained ourselves over the centuries by using religion as a coping mechanism.

In order to understand the importance of religion in the lives

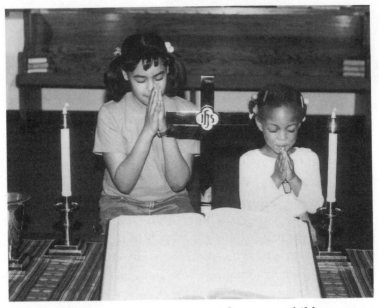

Spiritual training is important for young children.

of most African Americans, it is necessary to look back at our beginnings in this country. Religion offered enslaved African Americans hope for a brighter tomorrow. The black preacher declared that there was a better day coming and a chance for freedom beyond earthly bondage. And though most people no longer care to hear "pie-in-the-sky sermons," it was those sermons that kept many people hanging on and believing that freedom and refuge would come someday.

While slave masters used religion and the selection of specific scriptures to try to control their slaves, the slaves were wise enough to use the scriptures to preach deliverance for themselves.

Today's Black Worship Experience

African American people enjoy a unique worship experience. The gregarious and celebrative worship style found in most black congregations is similar to worship styles found in several traditional west African religious practices. Ours is a mix of African and American cultures that is structured to meet the unique needs that are inherent in the lives of African Americans.

The United States Constitution allows its citizens the right to choose any form of worship or none at all. The majority of African Americans have chosen to embrace traditional Christian practices of worship. One fairly recent and interesting phenomenon has been the Afrocentric Christian worship approach. This approach emphasizes pride in heritage and is constructed around a liberation theology.

While most African Americans continue to follow a Christian tradition of worship, a growing number of African Americans has embraced other religions such as Islam and Buddhism. Whatever religious path you have chosen, there is a strong chance that you seek guidance, comfort and a sense of purpose in life through the worship of a Supreme Being or God Force.

Most great religions have common threads such as compassion and the sacredness of human life. Whatever your religious affiliation, it is probably your way of being connected to a higher being and an ongoing effort to reach a higher level of thinking, living and interacting with your fellow human beings.

Whatever religious affiliation you choose, recognize that it is one of the best ways to undergird the moral values that you would like to see in your children. Children are fascinated by things spiritual and are full of questions about religious beliefs and practices. This is your opportunity to share your religious beliefs and spiritual views with them.

> Go within every day and find the inner strength so that the world will not blow your candle out.
> — *Katherine Dunham*

While you may have a sense of spiritual connectedness, hundreds of thousands of children grow up never having attended a religious service. Children who have some spiritual base have additional support other than what you are able to provide. Life is too complex and difficult for you to sustain yourself and your children. They will need other ways to cope with some of the harsher realities of life, and having fundamental religious beliefs is one way to increase their coping skills.

> In the beginning God, . . . in the end God. —
> *Desmond Tutu*

Hopefully children that are given religious instruction will use that instruction to seek a higher plane of spirituality in life.

Children who have a spiritual background will understand the sanctity of life. They will not harm, rob, steal and kill other human beings. As they grow and develop, so can their spiritual base if you continue to guide and encourage the spiritual connection.

Seven Practices to Foster a Spiritual Anchor in Your Family

1. Attend religious services with some regularity.
2. Read from books that undergird the fundamentals of your religious beliefs, such as The Bible and The Koran.
3. Set aside time for weekly family devotion and prayer.
4. Meditate to find that quiet inner place of peace.
5. Foster association with others who share your religious beliefs.
6. Observe the oneness of mankind and seek to practice a belief in equality.
7. Seek ways to put your spiritual beliefs into practice by doing for others. This can be an individual or group cause. It can be financial and participatory.

There is no end to finding ways to help others, from sharing information to serving in a homeless shelter.

The Importance of Holidays and Celebrations

All people have customs and traditions that include celebrations commemorating events that are important to their past and hold significance for the present and future. African Americans are no different. Besides celebrating the official holidays of the nation, such as Presidents' Day, Easter, Independence Day, Labor Day, Veterans' Day, Thanksgiving, and Christmas, African Americans celebrate special events that are uniquely important to them.

We must celebrate events of special significance for several reasons. The ceremony and pomp that accompany such celebrations are in place not only to raise awareness of the event historically, but to maintain its present and future importance. To secure meaningful and healthy tradition, it becomes the responsibility of parents to observe special holidays and celebrations with their children. This enables children to grasp the significance of past struggles, understand the importance of building community and prepare to take their places in the grand scheme of unfolding events.

African American Holidays and Celebrations

Martin Luther King, Jr., Holiday. His January 15th birthday was finally declared a national holiday in 1986. This was not an easy accomplishment. Coretta Scott King, her family, Stevie Wonder, and a host of others were unrelenting in their efforts to see that Dr. King's birthday become a national holiday.

African American History Month. February is a monthlong celebration of African American History and Culture. Carter G. Woodson established Negro History Week in 1926 to commemorate the achievements and contributions of African Americans. [See p. 94]

Juneteenth Celebrations occur in several states. This holiday was established to commemorate the emancipation of many slaves that were still in bondage long after the signing of the Emancipation Proclamation in January 1863. At that time, word traveled slowly across the United States. In many cases it was June or later before many enslaved people realized that they had been set free. This event that occurred just a little over a century ago is certainly something worth shouting about.

Kwanzaa. The African American Holiday of Kwanzaa is the brainchild of Dr. Maulana Karenga, an eminent professor and authority on African history. He created Kwanzaa to reaffirm, restore and celebrate African culture, family, community and heritage. Dr. Karenga recognized the need for African Americans to rally around a sense of community, thus the development of the Nguzo Saba which consist of seven principles in order to rebuild and strengthen ourselves. Kwanzaa began in 1966 and is celebrated December 26–January 1. The understanding of Kwanzaa continues to grow as more and more African Americans participate in this communal celebration to promote values, encourage common identity, purpose and direction. It is interesting to note that Kwanzaa is the only communal celebration among African American people. All other holidays celebrated by African Americans are organized around the lives of heroines and heroes.

Kwanzaa celebrations continue to grow as individuals, families, organizations, and churches join together the last week of the year to affirm one another and to lay the mental plans to build community.

Though purely an African American celebration, Kwanzaa is founded on principles and attitudes that are prevalent in many African societies. These principles facilitate our ability to look at where we are now and how to meet the challenges that are ahead.

The *Nguzo Saba* (Seven Principles)

1. UMOJA (unity) — To strive for and maintain unity in the family, community, nation and race.
2. KUJICHAGULIA (Self-determination) — To define ourselves, name ourselves, create for ourselves and speak for ourselves instead of being defined, named created for and spoken for by others.
3. UJIMA (Collective Work and Responsibility) — To build and maintain our community together and make our sister's and brother's problems our problems and to solve them together.
4. UJAMAA (Cooperative Economics) — To build and main-

tain our own stores, shops and other businesses and to profit from them together.

5. NIA (Purpose) — To make our collective vocation the building and developing of our community in order to restore our people to their traditional greatness.

6. KUUMBA (Creativity) — To do always as much as we can, in the way we can, in order to leave our community more beautiful and beneficial than we inherited it.

7. IMANI (Faith) — To believe with all our heart in our people, our parents, our teachers, our leaders and the righteousness and victory of our struggle.

CHAPTER SEVENTEEN

Lessons to Help Us

There are lessons in life that are best learned through experience. Lessons can also be learned by observing how other people go about their daily lives.

Though they may be applied in school settings, many of life's most important lessons are not necessarily a part of any school curriculum. The right of teaching children many of the more profound lessons in life belongs to parents, extended family, and other caregivers entrusted with their well-being.

Listed below are 54 simple but fundamental lessons that can help those who are engaged in the joy and challenge of shaping young lives. This list is by no means complete. It is just a beginning list for parents and guardians to read, then expand and build upon, as they devise creative ways to teach your children—our children—about life.

Even with our best efforts, guiding our children is difficult at times. If you do not believe in the fundamentals yourself, only half-heartedly practice some of them, it will be even harder for you to teach them to your children.

The effort may prove a gratifying, yet frightening and humbling experience. Yet, I am convinced it is worth the effort to try to teach these lessons that translate into building good character and a strong, healthy value system in our young.

Important Lessons To Teach Your African American Child

1. There Is a God. This God or God Force is greater than you or I. How human beings all over the world relate to this God Force varies. They will, in time, develop their own unique relationship with the God Force. The God Force is positive, never negative. There are other forces in existence, but none as great as the God Force.

2. You Are One of a Kind. There is no one else in the whole wide world that is exactly the same as you are. This uniqueness makes each of us special. Being aware of our unique characteristics can serve as a positive force in our lives. It is important to respect and appreciate the uniqueness of others.

3. The Mind, Body and Spirit Must Be Properly Cared for. The mind is our connection to the world around us. As we take in and process new information, we stimulate our minds to soar to higher heights. The more we seek to develop our brain power, the more we will realize what a wonderfully complex computer that we carry around with us. The mind is capable of great things if we seek challenges continually. How we use our mind will determine whether we soar with eagles or keep our feet in the mud.

Good health habits will help maintain a strong healthy body. We reap the rewards of taking care of our bodies properly when we reach middle age and beyond. Proper diet, exercise and rest are essential to maintaining good health. Substances and habits that offend the body diminish our health and strength.

The spirit is the essence of our very being. It defines us as human beings and as much more than flesh and blood. It moves us beyond physical boundaries and into dimensions that allow us to move to higher levels of thinking and action.

4. Respect the Earth. The earth is our home. Since it is the only home we will ever have, then it is important to observe, respect, study and take care of our planet. Everything that we have and use is a by-product of the earth. We must guard and protect the earth and participate in keeping it in proper balance.

5. Be Honest. Honesty is still the best policy. In all matters, strive to be an honest person. Honesty means adhering to high standards of integrity in all of your dealings with others.

6. Be Responsible. Being responsible means following through on matters of obligation. Whether it is learning to do chores without constant prodding, feeding the dog, doing homework or keeping a promise to a friend, taking responsibility for your actions is imperative. Responsibilities increase with age, so the earlier children learn to accept small responsibilities, the easier for them as they move toward adult responsibilities. Many individuals who have everything going for them, including superior intellect, are not successful nor are as successful as they could be because they shun responsibility.

> My concept of happiness is to be fulfilled in a spiritual sense.
> — *Coretta Scott King*

7. Be Punctual. Very few people are always on time for everything all of the time. Too many people are always late for everything all of the time. Punctuality is a good habit to have. Remember, bad habits are easily formed and one of the worst ones that many of us are guilty of is tardiness. Is it necessary to be late or is it just your bad habit? Many people have "missed the boat" because they are not punctual.

8. Maintain a Positive Attitude. Teach your child that centering on positive forces will enable him to move forward and live life more fully.

Maintaining a positive attitude every hour, seven days a week, three hundred sixty-five days a year is more than most of us can do. However, we can maintain a positive attitude much of the time. Everyone has low moments in life, even children. Children have matters that concern them just as adults do. We tend to minimize children's problems because they are young. But remember, the problem that a child faces is in direct proportion to his world. A child is not an adult with adult answers. Encourage them to think positively because part of the solution to a concern or problem may be in one's ability to think it through so that a positive outcome can be reached. Teach children that when you reach a very low point, the next move is up.

9. Be Cordial. Being cordial toward people usually proves to be a big asset. Speak first. Don't wait around to see if someone is going to speak to you first. There are too many real concerns in the world than to be caught up in pettiness. You lose nothing by being cordial or friendly. Reaching out to others and being cordial makes the world a better place. Speaking to someone or sharing a smile may lift someone who has a broken spirit.

10. Every Human Being Has Worth. Teach your child that all human beings have worth. Worth is not tied to her economic station in life, family background, racial designation, material possessions or physical characteristics. Rather, worth is tied to her character. She should be taught that she is not less than any other human being on the face of the earth.

11. Every Human Being Has Strengths. Every human being has strong points. Having strength in one area or another does not make one person superior to another. It means that they have a talent to do something very well. Wise people recognize their strengths, develop their strengths and use them to their advantage.

12. Every Human Being Has Weaknesses. For all the strengths that we possess, every person has weaknesses. It is wise to not be judgmental because we will not want to be judged harshly for our own weaknesses. Perhaps tolerance for others may enable someone to overcome a weakness.

13. Be Yourself. A part of being a unique creation means that you will have your own distinct personality, mannerisms and idiosyncrasies. Appreciate and accept your uniqueness. When children are taught to accept themselves, they soon find that others are more accepting of them.

14. Be Polite. "Thank You," "Please," and "May I" are never inappropriate and should be used frequently. Showing gratitude and appreciation will always be in vogue. Those who seldom use such words are considered ill-trained, ill-mannered and rude.

15. Respect Others' Property. You value your possessions. So do others. No one wants their possessions trashed or abused. Treat other people's possessions as though they belong to you.

16. Associate with Positive People. You are judged by the company that you keep. Associate with other young people who have goals in mind. People who are negative and have no goals will soon wear you down. Seek out people who are upbeat and are going places. Friends influence us. Choose them carefully.

17. Know That Everyone Makes Mistakes. Children need to understand that no one is perfect. We all have shortcomings. Though everyone makes mistakes, it is wise to be aware when you have made a mistake and even wiser to try not to repeat the same mistake. Some types of mistakes that we make in life are more costly than others.

18. Spend Some Time Alone. Some people are much more comfortable spending time alone than others, while some of us prefer a crowd around all the time. Yet, it is good to have some time alone so that one can be introspective. Being alone with one's thoughts can be rejuvenating. Being alone allows time for reflection on what has transpired. Solitude also allows time to look toward the future.

19. Save. It is easier for young children to learn to save than it is for grownups who have never developed the habit of saving. Children can learn to put a small portion of their money in the bank. If they are taught to save a little of their allowance and to save a few dollars from doing little chores, before long they will understand how their little stash will grow.

20. Avoid Borrowing. Children should be taught early to avoid borrowing. Many a friendship has been shattered by borrowing and lending. Borrowing is often the line of least resistance. It is better to try to get what you need independent of others. Do you know someone who "borrows" but never returns anything? If they do return a borrowed item, it is not in the same condition as when you lent it. If you must borrow, return the item promptly and in good repair. If you damage a borrowed item, own up to it and pay for or replace it. If you need to borrow money, go to a bank.

21. Be Self-reliant. Toddlers are making an effort to be self reliant when they first struggle to dress themselves even though they may put shoes on the wrong feet and pants on backward. Build on this effort at independence by allowing children to do for themselves the things they are able to. People who lean on others are very pathetic when the props are pulled out from under them. People who learn to be self reliant accomplish more, enjoy a higher degree of independence and feelings of self worth.

22. Be Purposeful. Even young children have a purpose to their activities. When children play games, they are doing more than having a good time, they are learning in the process. Having a purpose means setting short and long range goals. Some little people have very big goals. As children grow mentally and physically, they are less likely to be a discipline problem at home or school if they are busy working toward their goals.

23. Share. Children can be taught to share within the family. They can share toys, games and treats. They can be taught to share their ideas and talents with others. Having a giving spirit brings joy and satisfaction.

24. Learn Something New Every Day. Life is a wonderful adventure if we are tuned in to all of the things around us. Help your child to understand that learning is a lifelong process. It is not limited to a classroom. Indeed, much of what we learn will not come from a structured classroom. Knowledge brings strength and freedom while ignorance keeps us in the dark.

25. Avoid Gossip. People who gossip a great deal usually developed the habit when they were young. When we gossip, we are using our tongues as deadly weapons. Children need to be taught that gossip is a negative trait. Being nosey about other people's affairs is unwise. Our time is always better spent keeping our own affairs in order.

26. Appreciate Your African Heritage. This was determined by the Supreme Being or Godforce. Although almost all African Americans are of mixed blood, their roots are African. Those African roots enabled their great grandparents, grandparents and parents to survive. Recognizing, understanding and appreciating this African legacy can be a strong foundation to build on.

27. Don't Waste Time on Bigots. If anyone has a problem with your child's African racial heritage, make sure that your child understands that that person has the problem, not your child.

There is no such thing as a "pure" race of people. All people have the blood of other races in their veins. According to the most current anthropological findings, we are all descendants of Mother Africa.

28. Have a Forgiving Spirit. Holding grudges is using energy negatively. Everyone offends someone at some point in time. Try to resolve the problem and move on. This does not mean letting someone use you for a doormat, nor does it mean you should allow repeated offenses. Sometimes it is necessary to keep a distance from someone who exhibits aggressive behavior or takes out their frustrations on you.

Life is short and there is much to do, therefore no one should wastes time rutted down in dealing with an old problem or offense. We must use our time and energy positively. Forgive, forget and move on.

29. Be Politically Aware. Being aware of the political systems that run the nation is an important way to make gains, individually and collectively. Local, state and national government is to be run by and for the people. If the citizenry refuses to be involved, then opportunists and shysters will run it for them. The outcome will not be good.

30. Vote. Democratic governments are shaped by the will of the people. The people exercise that will by use of the vote. If you do not vote, you have no voice. African Americans must remain aware of the price that has been paid for their voting rights. Many of our ancestors were beaten and murdered trying to exercise the right to vote. Their blood cries out from the grave when we sit at home on election days.

31. Be a Good Communicator. Communication skills can be taught early. A good communicator recognizes the importance of listening as well as speaking. People who communicate well must first be good listeners. Active listeners tune into what others are saying and acknowledge that they are listening. Poor listeners hardly hear what others are saying. They are just waiting for their turn to speak.

32. Think for Yourself. He who controls your mind, controls you. Use all available resources and information to understand issues and events. From this draw your own conclusions. Be in control of your own mind.

33. Be Willing To Stand Alone. The majority is not always right. In truth, it is often wrong or off-base. When you recognize truth, stand by your convictions. Standing alone is not easy, but it has its own satisfaction when you have the courage of your convictions. Remember the majority used the law to say that black Americans had no rights. It was only when a few small voices were willing to speak out and stand up for their convictions that changes came about.

34. Don't Try To Be Responsible for Others' Actions. African Americans are often heard making statements that imply that they must somehow carry the weight of the whole race on their two little narrow shoulders. No individual can nor should be held responsible for someone else's actions just because they happen to share the same racial background.

We must get rid of the practice of feeling personally responsible for the actions of the deviant members of our race. It is important to speak out against wrong, no matter the race of the perpetrator. Take the time to point out to your children those who exhibit aberrant behavior.

People of other races seldom feel personally responsible for the deviant actions of members of their race because they are not. Neither should we feel a personal sense of guilt for those among our race who are pathological. Trying to carry the weight of an entire race is counterproductive and impossible.

35. Never Give Up. When there are goals to reach, and there always are, then there will be mountains to climb, valleys to cross and oceans to swim. Our forefathers ran many obstacle courses successfully. Though our obstacle courses may be different, we must find ways to run them successfully. It is only when we persevere to reach our goals that we will enjoy success and advancement. Many obstacles may be placed in your path and a course may have to be altered, but we must never give up.

36. Respect All People. People who are different from you are not more or less because of their differences. The world is made up of diverse groups, and unfortunately many of these diverse groups refuse to acknowledge the humanity of others who are different from them. This lack of tolerance created the horrors in Bosnia, Botswana and Rwanda. Everyone gains when a spirit of cooperation prevails and everyone loses when some groups refuse to recognize the humanity of others.

37. Avoid Racial Slurs, Jokes, and Stereotypes. Racial slurs, ethnic jokes and stereotypes all have one purpose, to demean the people that they are used against. There purpose is to make those who are the objects of such attacks a little less human than those who engage in the practice. Children should be taught not to utter them nor to stand still and be the victim of such actions. They are always within their rights to speak out in protest, whether there are two, three or a crowd present.

38. Make Decisions. Children who are allowed to make small decisions, will be better able to make decisions on more complicated matters as they mature. Decisions should be made on current knowledge, information available and the best judgment that one has. Not choosing a course of action is a form of making a decision to do nothing. Do something.

39. Cry When You Need to. Contrary to a widely held belief, crying is not necessarily a sign of weakness. Crying is an important emotion. It helps us stay in touch with our feelings. It is very important for males and females to be able to shed tears. A good cry can help us come to terms with our emotions and move us toward necessary action.

40. Laugh Often. In fact laugh a lot. It has been proven scientifically that people who laugh lower their stress levels. It is good for the spirit and good for others who are around you. Many

Give children a chance to
develop all their talents.

times a good sense of humor and a good laugh will pull you through when all else fails.

41. Have Pride In Our Past. African American people can take pride in our past. We have a past filled with inventions and discoveries. We have a past filled with acts of valor and heroism. Our past has been about a people who were survivors. This resilient spirit has been passed to us. It is up to us to build upon the strength of the ancestors.

As we move toward the twenty-first century, African Americans should have some knowledge of the myriad contributions that our people have made, from the oldest university in the world in Cairo, Egypt (Al-Azhar) to hundreds of inventions in the United States.

42. Recognize the Value of Education. Our forefathers knew that an education was valuable, even when they didn't have any. They knew that education holds wonderful secrets. Why else would their oppressors go to great lengths to make certain that they did not get an education. Getting a solid educational foundation is the primary step to success. Children should be taught of our struggle to get an education in the past. This should be used as motivation to move them toward achieving at the highest educational levels within their ability. Prepare well, then when opportunity knocks, they'll be ready.

43. Support African American Organizations. Give generously of your money, talents and time to black organizations that are working to improve the quality of life for black people. Organizations cannot function on your good wishes. They need our financial assistance and whatever expertise we have to offer.

44. Choose Dates and Mates Based on Respect. Why would anyone date or marry someone that she does not respect or that does not respect her? What a waste of time. It doesn't take long to know if you have anything in common with another individual in terms of values and goals in life. Use your personal measure to decide the level of the relationship or if there should be a relationship at all.

45. **Support Black Businesses.** Much of our future success will depend upon our own economic empowerment. He who controls the pursestrings, controls. We have yet to learn to harness and use our more than $400 billion wisely. We will make rapid advancement when we learn to support black enterprises.

46. **Keep Your Word.** Your word is a reflection of a weak or a strong character. Too many people will commit to anything and make any promise without a thought as to what they are doing. It is very hard to respect people who do not keep their word. If you say you will do something, do it. If you do not wish to do something, say "NO." The word "NO" can be a form of positive assertiveness as opposed to saying "YES" to everything, then breaking your promises.

47. **Question Authority.** When children feel the need, they should be able to ask questions. They should not be taught to accept commonly held beliefs as absolutes. By questioning, they will learn faster and form opinions based on knowledge that they gain by being inquisitive. What would our present world be like if brave individuals like Mahatma Gandhi, Martin Luther King, Jr., and Nelson Mandela had not questioned the status quo?

48. **Respect Elders.** In African society, elders are revered for their knowledge and wisdom. Africans understand that wisdom can only come from long years of living. Unfortunately, American society tends to disregard or cast aside its elder citizens. This society has been unwilling to sit at the feet of elder citizens and learn. Find a way to have your children in the presence of older members of our society.

49. **Learn to Work with Your Hands.** Children should be taught that any honest work should be respected. No matter how financially secure that some people seem to be, there was a time not long ago when someone in their family labored with their hands. Having skilled hands can save you a great deal of money if you are able to repair or build things. Working with your hands is also therapeutic. People who are in mental institutions are often asked to make things with their hands because of the healing value

of using the hands. Take pride in the ability to use your hands.

Black Americans used their hands to help build the United States. From picking cotton to digging ditches, to building buildings, we provided the backbreaking labor that helped build a nation and keep it running. Never be ashamed of honest work, no matter how physical. Too many young African Americans are taught to disdain any physical labor. No wonder some engage in a life of crime for the quick buck.

50. Be Willing To Say, "I'm Sorry." If anyone were perfect, he would never need to say the words, "I'm sorry." Since no one is perfect, then those are words that everyone should learn to say when appropriate. Everyone makes mistakes. Big people are able to apologize. Small people seldom or never do.

51. Seize Opportunity. Opportunity may knock more than once, but why take a chance on waiting for the second or third knock? Prepare well, be the best that you can be and when opportunity comes, you will be ready. Seize the moment. Should have, could have and would have will not propel you to where you wish you had gone.

52. Don't Be Rigid. Teach children not to argue people down who do something in a different manner than they do. There are many ways to do the same thing. Because you do something a certain way does not mean that that is the only way to accomplish the task at hand. Observe how other people do the same task. It may prove to be a very positive learning experience.

53. Be Generous with Compliments. It is good to acknowledge positive qualities that other people have. Children who are complimented, usually learn to be very positive and complimentary toward others. Teach them to accept compliments graciously.

The habit of being ungracious and critical usually begins in childhood. Jealous children grow into jealous adults. These individuals are pathetic as they go about finding fault with everyone else. They are quick to point out the shortcomings of others, but seldom recognize their own.

54. Remain Hopeful. Believing that you can accomplish

anything is a wonderful beginning. Let us point young African Americans toward the stars. Time is limited and shorter than young children are able to realize. Yet, as caring loving parents and guardians of their future, we must teach children to keep hope and to use their time wisely.

As long as they believe they can, then they will. Looking back at the brave and illustrious record of the ancestors will enable us to teach African American children to keep hope. If African American children keep hope they can dream big dreams, work hard, persevere and move forward toward the fulfillment of their dreams.

EPILOGUE

One thing I truly believe and hold strong convictions about is the ability of African American children to succeed.

In the African American child lies all the God-given gifts and talents that all other children possess. As with all children, their gifts and talents must be awakened, nurtured and developed to the highest potential.

If they are given guidance, they will move in positive directions.

If they are taught, they will learn.

If they are dealt with in a positive manner, they will move toward the positive.

If they are placed in competitive situations, they will compete vigorously and triumph.

If they are received and accepted in school, they will view education positively.

If they are challenged academically at a young age, they will excel.

If they are nurtured and loved, they will love themselves. And by learning to love themselves, they will strongly believe in themselves and in their ability to accomplish great things.

If they are taught to love and respect African American people, they will; and that love and respect will be transmitted to all people.

They must be taught to view the history of African American people in terms of survivorship, resilience and strength, thereby giving them a great legacy upon which to build.

If parents, caregivers, educators, religious and community institutions will hold high expectations for African American children, properly nurture and love them and give them the tools that they need, then they will meet and, often, exceed challenges placed before them.

I believe in African American children. They are capable of great things and deserve nothing less than our best efforts.

The Joy and Challenge of Raising African American Children has found its way into your hands for a reason. It is offered to the entire village as a charge to guide children toward the light and in positive directions. Let us form a circle of love around our Golden Fruit, accept the challenge joyfully and "March on 'til victory is won!"

❖

SECTION V

Resources

RESOURCES:

Historical Points of Special Interest

Experience a whole new world by traveling and exploring various sites of special interest to African Americans. There is a growing interest in preserving and restoring sites and artifacts pertaining to African American life.

Many African American families make annual pilgrimages to various historical points. Join this growing number of African American families who are determined to discover more about their roots, history and ancestors.

Some of the sites listed below are found in guides like the excellent *Hippocrene U.S.A. Guide to Black America* by Marcella Thum (New York: Hippocrene Books). Begin with this list and expand to include other sites as you read, travel, and explore with your family.

ALABAMA

■ W. C. Handy Home and Museum, 620 West College Street, Florence, AL 35630. Handy was known as "The Father of the Blues."

■ Civil Rights Memorial, Southern Poverty Law Center, 400 Washington Avenue, Montgomery, AL 36104. Names and honors martyrs of the civil rights movement.

■ Dexter Avenue King Memorial Baptist Church, 454 Dexter Avenue, Montgomery, AL 36104. The Montgomery Bus Boycott was organized here on December 2, 1955. Dr. Martin Luther King, Jr., was pastor 1954-59.

■ Slavery Library, Talladega College, Talladega, AL 35160, contains the Amistad Murals of slaves and their leader, Cinque, who led the mutiny on the slaveship, the Amistad.

■ The Oaks, home of Booker T. Washington, Tuskegee Institute National Historic Site, Tuskegee, AL 36088, was built by students. They also designed and built the original buildings on campus.

■ George Washington Carver Museum, Tuskegee Institute National Historic Site, Tuskegee, AL 36088 contains a replica of Carver's early laboratory.

ARKANSAS

■ Central High School,1500 Park Street, Little Rock, AR 72202. In the fall of 1957, nine African American students had to be escorted into the school by federal troops in order to desegregate Central High School.

CALIFORNIA

■ Beckwourth Pass, on CA 70 just east of the junction with U.S. 395. James Beckwourth found this pass through the Sierra Nevada Mountains in 1850.

■ California Afro-American Museum, 600 State Drive, Los Angeles, CA 90037.

■ Museum of African American Art, 4005 Crenshaw Blvd., Los Angeles, CA 90008.

■ Ebony Museum of Art, 1034 14th Street, Oakland, CA 94606.

■ San Francisco African American Historical and Cultural Society, Fort Mason Center, Building C, Buchanan and Marina Blvd., San Francisco, CA 94123.

COLORADO

■ Black American West Museum and Heritage Center, 3091 California Street, Denver, CO 80205. Houses artifacts of the early black pioneers.

CONNECTICUT

■ Harriet Beecher Stowe House, 73 Forest Street, Hartford, CT 06105. She is author of Uncle Tom's Cabin.

■ Connecticut Afro-American Historical Society, 444 Orchard Street, New Haven, CT 06511

■ Tri-sided Sculpture of Senge Pieh, a.k.a. Joseph Cinque. Sculpture tells story of Cinque as Mendi farmer in Africa, on trial in New Haven and preparing to set sail to his native land.

DELAWARE

■ Wilmington Afro-American Historical Society, 512 East 4th Street, Wilmington, DE 19801

DISTRICT OF COLUMBIA

■ Benjamin Banneker Circle and Fountain, L'Enfant Promenade and Maine Avenue. Banneker helped survey and plan the layout of the nation's capital.

■ Bethune Museum and Archives, 1318 Vermont Avenue, N.W., Washington, DC 20005. Home of Mary McLeod Bethune, founder of Bethune-Cookman College, National Council of Negro Women and advisor to presidents.

■ Emancipation Proclamation, Library of Congress. Freed slaves in states not occupied by federal troops.

- Cedar Hill, 1411 W Street, S.E., Washington, DC 20020. Home of Frederick Douglass, former slave who became great orator and champion of rights for slaves and freedmen.
- National Museum of African Art, 950 Independence Avenue, S.W., Washington, DC 20024. African Art of sub-Sahara Africa.
- National Museum of American History, on Constitution Avenue between 12th and 14th Streets, N.W. Second floor contains exhibit of the great African American migration from the south, 1915-1940.

FLORIDA
- Bethune-Cookman College, 640 Second Avenue, Daytona Beach, FL 32114. Home of Mary McLeod Bethune.
- Eatonville, Florida, is the oldest completely African American community in the United States. Home of black author Zora Neale Hurston, of "Their Eyes Were Watching God" fame.
- Black Archives History and Research Foundation, 5400 N.W. 22nd Avenue, Miami, FL 33142.
- Black Archives Research Center and Museum, Florida A & M University, Tallahassee, FL 32307.

GEORGIA
- Martin Luther King, Jr., National Historic Site, 449 Auburn Avenue, N.E., Atlanta, GA 00000, includes boyhood home, church, burial site, reflecting pool, chapel, archives building, and Martin Luther King, Jr., Center for Nonviolent Social Change.
- Ebenezer Baptist Church, 407 Auburn Avenue, N.E., Atlanta, GA 30312. Martin Luther King, Jr., was associate pastor.
- Morehouse College, 830 Westview Drive, S.W., Atlanta, GA 30314. Martin Luther King, Jr., is the school's most famous alumnus. His statue stands in front of King International Chapel.
- Uncle Remus Museum, U.S. 441 in Turner Park, Eatonton, GA 31024. The home of Alice Walker, author of *The Color Purple*, is also in Eatonton.
- Harriet Tubman Historical and Cultural Museum, 340 Walnut Street, Macon, GA 31201.

ILLINOIS
- Du Sable Museum of African American History, 740 E. 56th Place, Chicago, IL 60637.
- Johnson Publishing Company, 820 S. Michigan Ave., Chicago, IL 60605. Home of *Ebony*, *Jet* and other black publications.

■ Katherine Dunham Museum, 1005 Pennsylvania, East St. Louis, IL 62205. Advanced black dance through the Katherine Dunham Dance Company.

INDIANA
■ Children's Museum, 3000 N. Meridian Street, Indianapolis, IN 46208. Fifth floor, exhibit area of African-American Scientists and Inventors from A to Z.

KANSAS
■ First National Black Historical Society of Kansas, 601 N. Water, Wichita, KS 67203.

KENTUCKY
■ Emma Reno Connor Black History Gallery, 602 Hawkins Drive, Elizabethtown, KY 42701.

■ Kentucky Horse Park, 4089 Iron Works Pike, Lexington, KY 40511. Burial Site of Isaac Murphy, black jockey who won three Kentucky Derbies.

LOUISIANA
■ Amistad Research Center, 6823 St. Charles Street, New Orleans, LA 70118. Houses the largest American ethnic historical archives in the world.

■ Black Heritage Tours, 4635 Touro Street, New Orleans, LA 70122.

MAINE
■ John Brown Russwarm Afro-American Center, 6-8 College Street, Brunswick, ME 04011, is the Little-Mitchell House, a stop on the Underground Railroad.

MARYLAND
■ Banneker-Douglass Museum of Afro-american Life And History, 84 Franklin Street, Annapolis, MD 21401.

■ Black American Museum, 1769 Carswell Street, Baltimore, MD 21218.

■ Eubie Blake National Museum And Cultural Center 409 N. Charles Street, Baltimore, MD 21201.

■ Great Blacks In Wax Museum, 1601 E. North Avenue, Baltimore, MD 21213. Features over one hundred life-size, wax figures of black historic figures such as Harriet Tubman and Rosa Parks.

MASSACHUSETTS
■ African Meeting House, 8 Smith Court, Boston, MA 02114, is the oldest black church building still standing in the United States.

■ Museum of Afro-American History, at Abiel Smith School, 46 Joy Street, Boston, MA 02114.

■ Black Heritage Trail, a 1.5 mile walking tour, Boston.

■ Crispus Attucks Monument, Boston Common.

■ Museum of the National Center of Afro-American Artists, 300 Walnut Avenue, Boston, MA 02108.

MICHIGAN
■ Motown Museum, 2648 W. Grand Boulevard, Detroit, MI 48208.

MISSISSIPPI
■ Delta Blues Museum, 114 Delta Avenue, Clarksdale, MS 38614.

MISSOURI
■ Black Archives of Mid-America, 2033 Vine Street, Kansas City, MO 64108.

■ Negro Leagues Baseball Museum, in Vine Street Historic District, Kansas City, MO 64108.

■ Scott Joplin Residence, 2658 Delmar Blvd., St. Louis, MO 63103.

NEBRASKA
■ Great Plains Black Museum, 2213 Lake Street, Omaha, NE 68110. Exhibits on black cowboys and early black settlers.

NEW HAMPSHIRE
■ Amos Fortune Grave, in the Old Burying Ground in Jaffrey Center, Jaffrey, NH 03452

NEW JERSEY
■ Afro American Historical and Cultural Society, 1841 Kennedy Boulevard, Jersey City, NJ 07303.

■ African Arts Museum, 23 Bliss Avenue, Tenafly, NJ 07670.

NEW YORK
■ Afro Arts Cultural Center, 2192 Adam Clayton Powell, Jr. Blvd. New York, NY 10027

■ Center for African Art, 54 East 68th Street, New York, NY 10021

■ Harriet Tubman Home, 180-182 South Street, Auburn, NY 13021.

■ Fredrick Douglas Monument, Highland Park Bowl, Rochester, NY 14620.

■ Fredrick Douglas Grave, Mount Hope Cemetery, 79 Mount Hope Avenue, Rochester, NY 14620.

■ Kush Museum of African and African-American Art and Antiquities, 25 High Street, Buffalo, NY 14203.

NORTH CAROLINA

■ Afro-American Cultural Center, 401 N. Myers Street, Charlotte, NC 28202.

■ Mattye Reed African Heritage Center, North Carolina A & T State University, Greesboro, NC 27401.

■ North Carolina Central University Art Museum, Durham, NC 27707

OHIO

■ African American Museum, 1765 Crawford Road, Cleveland, OH 44106.

■ National Afro-American Museum and Cultural Center, 1350 Brush Row Road, Wilberforce, OH 45384.

■ Paul Laurence Dunbar Home, 219 N. Summit Street, Dayton, OH 45407.

OKLAHOMA

■ National Cowboy Hall of Fame and Western Heritage Center, 1700 N.E. 63rd Street, Oklahoma City, OK 73111.

■ Sanamu African Gallery, Kirkpatrick Center Museum Complex, 2nd Floor, 2100 Northeast 52nd Street, Oklahome city, OK 73111.

OREGON

■ Children's Museum, 3037 Southwest 2nd Avenue, Portland, OR 97201. Contains an authentic African village.

PENNSYLVANIA

■ Afro-American Historical and Cultural Museum, 7th and Arch Streets, Philadelphia, PA 19106.

■ Charles L. Blockson Afro-american Collection, Temple University Library, Broad Street and Montgomery Avenue, Philadelphia, PA 19121.

SOUTH CAROLINA

■ Oyotunji African Village, U.S. 17-21, Sheldon SC. 50 miles south of Charleston. The village is patterned after the ancient Yoruba tradition.

■ Slave Auction Building, 6 Chalmers Street Charleston, SC 29401.

TENNESSEE

■ Alex Haley House and Museum, 200 S. Church Street and Haley Avenue, Henning, TN 38401. Haley won the 1976 Pulitzer Prize for the novel *Roots*.

■ Beale Street Historic District, downtown off Riverside Drive, Memphis, TN. Bessie Smith and W.C. Handy were regular entertainers on Beale Street.

■ Fisk University and Carl Van Vechten Gallery of Fine Arts, 17th Avenue North, Nashville, TN 37203. On the second floor of the Fisk library there is an extensive collection of materials on the black man in Africa, America and the Caribbean. W.E.B. DuBois statue is also located on the Fisk campus.

■ Lorraine Motel, 406 Mulberry Street, Memphis, TN 38103. Dr. Martin Luther King, Jr., was assassinated on the balcony of this motel on April 4, 1968.

■ National Civil Rights Museum, at site of the Lorraine Hotel. Memphis, TN. Comprehensive overview of the Civil Rights Movement.

TEXAS

■ George Washington Carver Museum, 1165 Angelina Street, Austin, TX 78702. Exhibits on black history and culture. One section devoted to George Washington Carver.

■ Museum of African-American Life and Culture, 1620 1st Avenue, Fair Park, Dallas, TX 75210.

VIRGINIA

■ Alexandria Black History Resource Center, 638 N. Alfred Street, Alexandria, VA 22314.

■ Booker T. Washington National Monument, 20 miles southeast of Roanoke via VA. 116 south to Burnt Chimney, then VA 122 North.

■ Hampton University Museum, Hampton University County Street, Hampton, VA 23661. Houses one of the oldest collections of African art in this country. Home to Henry O. Tanner's "The Banjo Lesson." A statue of Booker T. Washington, Hampton University's most famous alumnus, is found here.

■ Jamestown Settlement, Jamestown, VA. Blacks were first brought here upon reaching America in 1619.

WEST VIRGINIA

Booker T. Washington Memorial Statue, located on grounds of the state capitol on Kanawha Blvd, Charleston, WV 25301.

WISCONSIN

■ America's Black Holocaust Museum, 2479 Martin Luther King Drive, Milwaulkee, WI 53208.

The Food Pyramid for Health

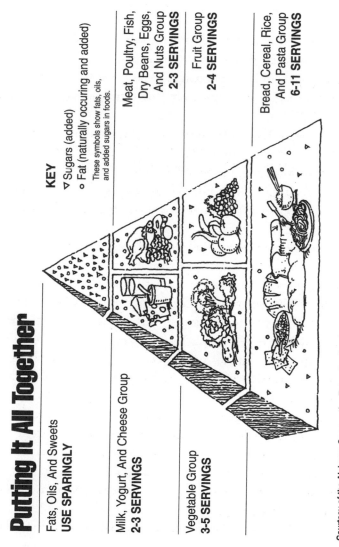

Putting It All Together

Fats, Oils, And Sweets
USE SPARINGLY

Milk, Yogurt, And Cheese Group
2-3 SERVINGS

Vegetable Group
3-5 SERVINGS

KEY
▽ Sugars (added)
○ Fat (naturally occuring and added)
These symbols show fats, oils,
and added sugars in foods.

Meat, Poultry, Fish,
Dry Beans, Eggs,
And Nuts Group
2-3 SERVINGS

Fruit Group
2-4 SERVINGS

Bread, Cereal, Rice,
And Pasta Group
6-11 SERVINGS

Courtesy of the Alabama Cooperative Extension Service

RESOURCES:

The World of Children's Books

Once upon a time, African American children had very little that they could relate to in literature books and school texts. In spite of not seeing themselves reflected in literature and other school texts, they still managed to learn from the texts and stories that were available.

Though they made do with what was available, the dirth of materials dealing with the black experience and black characters did little for the self-esteem of black children.

Few African Americans were encouraged to write, and those that did found getting published was extremely difficult, if not impossible.

In the nineties we find many different and more positive images than a few years ago. Several events brought about this change and put a new face on the world of children's books today.

In 1965, educator Nancy Larrick conducted a study and published the results in a *Saturday Review* article entitled "The All-White World of Children's Books." The startling findings were that only four-fifths of one percent of 5000 children's books published between 1962-64 included any information about African Americans.

Larrick's study bore fruit and today the number of good books with multicultural themes continues to grow at a steady clip. Publishers, bookstores, librarians and enlightened teachers have become increasingly aware that there is a need for, an interest in and a market for books by and about African Americans and other racial and ethnic groups.

In 1967, The Council on Interracial Books for Children

sponsored contests to encourage African American writers and illustrators, and today many of those participants are well-known writers of children's literature.

Larrick's study and the ensuing efforts of publishers and organizations that recognized the need for diversity in literature resulted in African American children finally having the opportunity to see themselves presented in books in a way that values them and their racial and cultural heritage.

As a parent or caregiver of African American children, it is extremely important that you select books that mirror your African American children. Their reading does not have to be restricted to African American books, but certainly, much of what they are introduced to at an early age should be about the lifestyles, culture and experiences of African American people.

Let's emphasize reading to our children starting at a very young age. We can feed their curiosity and whet their appetites to

Hook children on books, and you can worry less about them getting hooked on something else.

want to know more. Once they are hooked on books, they will retain an interest in reading throughout life.

By carefully selecting literature from a multicultural base, we will help children develop high self-esteem. Further, we will enhance their understanding of the past, help them appreciate the present and anticipate a bright future.

BOOKS WITH AFRICAN AMERICAN THEMES

Pre-School to Second Grade
A Is For Africa by Jean Carey Bond (Franklin Watts, 1969)
Abby by Jeanette F. Caines (Harper, 1973)
Afro-Bets Abc Book by Cheryl Hudson (Just Us Books, 1987)
An Enchanted Hair Style by Alexis De Veaux (Harper Collins, 1987)
Aunt Harriett's Railroad In The Sky by Faith Ringgold (Crown, 1992)
Grandpa's Face by Eloise Greenfield (Philomel/Putnam, 1986)
It Takes A Village by Jane Cowen-Fletcher (Scholastic, 1993)
More Than Anything Else by Marie Bradby (Orchard, 1995)
Why Mosquitos Buzz In People's Ears by Walter D. Myers (Parents Magazine Press, 1969)
Willie's Not The Huggin' Kind by Joyce Durham Barrett (Harper, 1989)

Grades Three and Four
Ashanti To Zulu by Margaret Musgrove (Dial, 1976)
Celebrating Kwanzaa by Diane Hoyt-Goldsmith (Holiday House, 1993)
Honey, I Love by Eloise Greenfield (Crowell, 1978)
The Hundred Penny Box by Sharon Bell Mathis (Viking, 1975)
Mufaro's Beautiful Daughters by John L. Steptoe (Lothrop, 1987)
Shake It To The One That You Love The Best by Cheryl W. Mattox (Warren-Mattox Productions, 1990)
Song Of The Trees by Mildred D. Taylor (Dial, 1975)
The Tiger Who Wore White Gloves by Gwendolyn Brooks (Third World, 1977)

Grades Four, Five and Six

Aida by Leontyne Price (Gulliver, 1990)

Black Pilgrimage by Thomas Feelings (Lothrop, 1972)

Black Women: A Salute To Black Inventors by Ann Chandler (Chandler White, 1992)

Cousins by Virginia Hamilton (Philomel, 1990)

The Dream Keeper And Other Poems by Langston Hughes (Knopf, 1986)

Go Free Or Die: A Story About Harriet Tubman by Jeri Ferris (Lerner/ Carolrhoda, 1988)

Johnnie: The Life Of Johnnie Rebecca Carr by Randall Williams (Black Belt, 1995)

Lift Every Voice And Sing by Il. Elizabeth Catlett (Walker & Co., 1993)

Mary Mcleod Bethune: Voice Of Black Hope by Milton Meltzer (Penguin/Puffin, 1988)

M. C. Higgins, The Great by Virginia Hamilton (Macmillan, 1974)

Grades Seven and Up

Blue Tights by Rita Williams-Garcia (Dutton/Lodestar)

Complete Works Of Paul Laurence Dunbar by Paul Laurence Dunbar (Dodd, 1914)

I Know Why The Caged Bird Sings by Maya Angelou (Bantam, 1970)

Outward Dreams: Black Inventors And Their Inventions by James S. Haskins (Walker, 1991)

Thurgood Marshall by Lisa Aldred (Chelsea House, 1990)

Touch Their Lives With Poetry

How beautiful are the words of a poet. How stimulating, powerful and thought provoking those words can be when put together in exotic, beautiful and plain patterns. The words of the poet draw out our deepest emotions. They can make us laugh, cry, chuckle and smile. Poetic words can cause us to be introspective.

African Americans have been writing poetry since little Phillis Wheatley was captured and brought to American shores in the seventeenth century. Yet long before Phillis was snatched from her home shores, African people knew the power and beauty of words. Griots memorized centuries of history of their people and waxed poetic genius in their powerful deliveries.

African Americans have continued this poetic succession right up to the present time. Our children can enjoy a rich inheritance from dozens of gifted poets. Such poets as Paul Laurence Dunbar, Countee Cullen and Langston Hughes ordained Gwendolyn Brooks, Rita Dove, Mari Evans, Imamu Baraka, Haki Madhubuti . . . They, in turn, will pass on the mantle to young black poets who will follow them.

African American writers and poets have told our story in verse and our children should be given the opportunity to hear that story from the pens of their own people. This experience can begin when children are toddlers and continue. Children will enjoy the rhythms of poetry just as much as they enjoy listening to parents and teachers read from juvenile books.

They should experience the joy of growing up with poetry. Poetry adds beauty and dimension to our lives. It helps us dream and yes, even daydream. Children who can dream will write their own success stories. Children who grow up listening to Dunbar's

Children who are taught to memorize poetry will have an enjoyable challenge and will strengthen their own verbal skills.

"Little Brown Baby" and Hughes's "The Dream Keeper" are much more likely to appreciate the sanctity of life and the potential of dreaming big dreams.

More power to the poets and to our children, our future poets. African American poets explore history, relish the present and look to the future. There are thousands of poems and hundreds of books of poetry on the market for your enjoyment. Add to this list many other poems that you and your children will enjoy reading aloud together. Offer them the challenge of memorizing some of their favorites.

Poems by African American Writers

And Still I Rise	Maya Angelou
By Myself	Eloise Greenfield
The Creation	James Weldon Johnson
The Dream Keeper	Langston Hughes
Dreams	Langston Hughes

Expectations	Emma M. Talbott
Feeling Good About Me	Charlotte M. Hill
Honey, I Love	Eloise Greenfield
Human Family	Maya Angelou
Lift Ev'ry Voice and Sing	James Weldon Johnson
Little Brown Baby	Paul Laurence Dunbar
Mother to Son	Langston Hughes
My People	Langston Hughes
The Negro Speaks of Rivers	Langston Hughes
We Real Cool	Gwendolyn Brooks
Who Can be Born Black	Mari Evans
Your World	Georgia Douglas Johnson

Poems by other poets that children will enjoy.

Equipment	Edgar Guest
Invictus	William Ernest Henley
The House by the Side of the Road	Samuel W. Foss
Keep A-Goin'	Frank L. Stanton
The Road Not Taken	Robert Frost
The Twenty-Third Psalm	David
See It Through	Edgar Guest
Stopping by Woods on a Snowy Evening	Robert Frost

RESOURCES:

Keeping The Negro Spiritual Alive

My great-grandmother, Susan Sangston Hammonds Miles, was enslaved until around the age of twenty. In her later years, she would sometimes share some of her experiences, both pleasant and sorrowful, with my mother. This resilient little lady, mother of twelve, who lived to be well over one hundred, told my mother about the slaves that would pass through the Bardstown-Bloomfield, Kentucky, area. As they were being taken to the deep south, Grandma Suze said that you could hear their sweet voices across the fields as they sang spirituals. She said it was the sweetest sound that she had ever heard.

It is fascinating to know that the beautiful Negro spirituals came out of such a mournful and painful time. I suspect that singing those beautiful, sometimes slow and sometimes spirited renditions and often in a minor key, kept many a slave hanging on and hoping for a better day.

No doubt the memory of those sweet voices, raised in hope, helped sustain my great-grandmother during a lifetime that exceeded a century.

We must keep the Negro Spiritual alive through our children. People of other races recognize the beauty and uniqueness of the Negro Spiritual, yet we have tended to ignore them and turned our ear only toward contemporary gospel.

> When I found I had crossed the line (to freedom), I looked at my hands to see if I was the same person. There was such a glory over everything. — *Harriet Tubman*

Our children should be taught to sing many of the spirituals that we have given to the world. Are you waiting on the schools to teach the Negro Spiritual? If they are to learn and appreciate them, they must hear the Spiritual at church and at home.

Listed here are just a few of the beautiful spirituals that African American people have given the world for enjoyment. You will find these in many church hymnals or you can ask a reference librarian to help you locate copies.

Couldn't Hear Nobody Pray
Deep River
Everytime I Feel the Spirit
Go Down, Moses
Great Day
He's Got the Whole World in His Hands
Hush! Hush!
I Shall Not Be Moved
It's Me
I've Got a Robe
Jesus Is a Rock in a Weary Land
Listen to the Lambs
Lord, I Want to Be a Christian
My Lord, What a Mourning!
No Hiding Place
Nobody Knows
O My Lord, What Shall I Do?
Oh, Freedom
Room Enough
Sit Down, Servant
Wade In the Water
Walk With Me
We Are Climbing Jacob's Ladder
Were You There?
When the Saints Go Marching In
Will the Lighthouse Shine on Me?
You Must Have That True Religion

RESOURCES:
Historically Black Colleges and Universities

Space does not permit here a listing of all the historically black colleges and universities in the U.S., but there are several readily available directories which list these schools. Two are:

Historically Black Colleges and Universities: Profiles of 91 Popular Schools—Proven Training Grounds for Tomorrow's Leaders (New Orleans: Wintergreen/Orchard House, Inc., 1995).

100 Best Colleges for African American Students (New York: Penguin USA, 1993).

Other directories are available at the reference desks of local libraries, as are guides to scholarships and other financial assistance.

ABOUT THE AUTHOR

Emma McElvaney Talbott is a writer and poet. She was an educator in the Jefferson County (Kentucky) school system for twenty-five years. She is still involved in education as a consultant for new teachers in the school district and teaches undergraduate-level courses in language arts.

Talbott has been a Louisville Courier-Journal Forum Fellow and writes book reviews and editorials for the *Courier-Journal*. She serves on several community boards that impact the lives of young people, such as the Chestnut Street Family YMCA.

She holds degrees from Kentucky State University and Indiana University, and has done postgraduate work at the University of Kentucky, University of Louisville, and Western Kentucky University leading to state certifications in school administration, supervision, and as a reading specialist.

She and her husband, Cecil, an engineer, are the parents of two sons. Chip (Cecil Jr.) a Stanford University and Georgia Tech graduate, is an engineer; and Chad, a Morehouse College and University of Georgia graduate, is an attorney.

Talbott is the youngest of six siblings. Playing the piano, taking long walks in the park, and playing tennis are her stress relievers.

This is her first book.